# 1,112 Down-to-Earth
# Garden Secrets

**Here are tips that really work—
from backyard gardeners
across the country!**

# Were you wondering about the answers to the questions on the cover? Here they are:

**My daughter keeps** rabbits out of her garden by digging a trench around the entire garden and filling it with the contents of her vacuum cleaner bag. To keep it from blowing away, she puts screening over it. There is enough scent of humans in this material to frighten off the rabbits.
—*Marlene Eveland, St. Thomas, Ontario*

**To protect our tomatoes** and peppers from late-season frost, we used plastic garbage bags tied to the plants' cages. They saved our crop this past year.
—*Paul and Marilyn Spencer, Davenport, Iowa*

**Use twist-ties** from garbage bags to help train vines to grow up a fence or trellis. Be sure to twist the ties loosely so there's plenty of room for the vines to grow.
—*Amber Wall, Hawthorne, Florida*

*And that's just the beginning—there are more than 1,100 garden secrets throughout this book for you to use in your backyard!*

# 1,112 Down-to-Earth
# Garden Secrets

### Here are tips that really work— from backyard gardeners across the country!

**Editors:** Julie Landry, Jeff Nowak

**Associate Editors:** Deb Mulvey, Jean Steiner, Sharon Selz, Mike Beno

**Consulting Horticulturist:** Melinda Myers

**Art Director:** Bonnie Ziolecki

**Illustrators:** Jim Sibilski, Tom Hunt, Gail Engeldahl

**Production:** Ellen Lloyd, Catherine Fletcher

**Editor, *Birds & Blooms* magazine:** Tom Curl

**Publisher:** Roy Reiman

*Birds & Blooms* Books
© 1998, Reiman Publications, L.P.
5400 S. 60th St., Greendale WI 53129
International Standard Book Number: 0-89821-233-2
Library of Congress Catalog Card Number: 98-65083
Printed in U.S.A.
Third Printing, March 2001

**Notice:** The information in this book has been gathered from a variety of people and sources, and all efforts have been made to ensure accuracy.

Remember, not every tip is suitable for every area of the country. We recommend having your soil tested by your state Extension Service or at a certified soil testing lab before acting on any information provided in this book.

Also, we've included a map of the U.S. Department of Agriculture hardiness zones on page 178. This will help you locate the approximate climate in which each contributor lives and will allow you to better assess if their advice will work in your backyard.

Reiman Publications assumes no responsibility for any injuries suffered or damages or losses incurred as a result of this information. All information should be carefully studied and clearly understood before taking any action based on the information or advice in this book.

Reiman Publications does not endorse or recommend any products mentioned in this book.

For your safety, read and follow all label directions when using commercial products and call your local utilities before digging in your yard.

**For additional copies of this book** or information on other books, write: *Birds & Blooms Books*, Suite 4540, P.O. Box 990, Greendale WI 53129. You can also order by phone and charge to your credit card by calling toll-free 1-800/558-1013. When ordering this book, ask for item 27015. Also mention Suite 4540.

# Foreword

I REALLY wish that I would have had this book when I first began working in the gardens of our company's yard 8 years ago.

Like the thousands of backyard "green thumbers" who contributed to this "hints" book, I, too, learned how to garden through trial and error (and trying a little of this and that which I picked up from other gardeners I talked to).

It took time, but eventually I discovered what was needed to make the grounds here at Reiman Publications the talk of the town. (They really are…our company's landscaping has become a landmark in Greendale, Wisconsin.)

So when the editors gave me a chance to preview the garden hints in this book, I couldn't help but think back to my first summer as the company "landlady", as Roy Reiman always refers to me.

I sure could have saved time using Liz McCain's idea for extending the blooming season. At planting time in her Florence, Oregon backyard, she alternates rows of flowers that bloom at different times.

And when I think about all the time I spent trying to keep the bedding plants from wilting just after I planted them…if I'd only had New York gardener Judy Weiss' suggestion that I soak their roots in a pail of water first to ease the shock.

### And Dealing with Critters…

There is the endless battle with the wildlife around here.

If I would have thought about using plastic Gutter Guard to protect my bedding impatiens the way Michelene Rocco of Lemont, Illinois does, we could have saved lots of young plants from hungry rabbits every summer.

And from Newark, Delaware, Weldon Burge's solution of removing the bottom of a Styrofoam cup and placing it over young plants to prevent damage from cutworms would have been mighty helpful, too.

Even though people around our place consider me an "expert gardener" (they make this assumption because we plant and maintain more than *35,000* bedding plants on our company's grounds each year), I've found many *new* tips in this book that I plan on trying. Here are just a few that made me say out loud…"Gee, why didn't I think of that?!"

**1.** Roses won't tolerate "wet feet", so check the drainage first. Before planting a rose, pour 2 gallons of water into the hole to make sure it will drain away in a few minutes. Great idea!

6

**2.** Morning glories will climb hollyhocks' sturdy stems and give your garden *double the color*. Why, sure!

**3.** To keep small tools close by, put a mailbox on a post near your garden. Saves lots of steps!

Why didn't I think of that simple mailbox idea before? I probably could have saved miles of walking back and forth to our storage shed for something I forgot.

### Filled with Over 1,100 Gardening "Secrets"

You'll find page after page of simple and practical gardening ideas like these in this book. If you're like me, you won't be able to put it down!

It's like having a conversation with more than 1,000 gardeners. They're down-to-earth people who would never think of keeping their tried-and-true tips to themselves. (I've even added a few tips of my own for you.)

I'm sure you're going to enjoy reading this book as much as I have. The tips in it will save hours and hours of experimenting in your gardens.

And that leaves more time to "stop and smell the roses"!

—*Gail Russell, "Landlady", Reiman Publications*

**JUST A FEW OF THE THOUSANDS.** Gail Russell (above left) maintains more than 35,000 bedding plants (like the ones below) in our company's backyard. Gail is a talented green thumb and is eager to try many of the garden secrets found in this book.

# CONTENTS

# CHAPTER ONE

# Spring:

# LET'S GET GROWING!

ENTHUSIASM RUNS high at the beginning of the growing season. And why shouldn't it? Plants will soon be taking root, and the following hints in this chapter are sure to get you and your garden off to a great start!

Whether it's coaxing your seeds to sprout, preparing the soil, strengthening your transplants or protecting your tender annuals from frost, here's a bushel of ideas that will make gardening even more enjoyable this year.

**When you're ready** to put down mulch, cover just-planted flowers with empty containers. (I use potting containers from newly planted shrubs.) You won't have to worry about covering the flowers with mulch or stepping on them.
*—Julie Ebelhar*
*Owensboro, Kentucky*

**Plastic cake** and cookie containers—like the ones you get from the bakery at the grocery store—make great places to start flowers from seed. The clear cover helps the seeds stay moist.  *—Jennie Tandy*
*Penetang, Ontario*

**Freezing parsley** seed will speed up germination.  *—Linde Foster*
*Worsley, Alberta*

**To sprout seeds**, rinse them in a small amount of water to which you've added a few drops of bleach. Fold a paper towel in quarters and dampen slightly. Scatter seeds on the towel and place in a zip-top bag.

Blow air into the bag through a straw. Keep in a dark place until roots appear, then transfer to starting pots. This is a great way for children to observe seeds sprouting, and only viable seeds get planted.
*—Betty Nichols*
*Laguna Beach, California*

**My husband** unrolls black plastic across the garden after it's prepared for planting. (Make sure soil is moist before covering.) We anchor it with bricks or dirt, punch holes in it and put in the plants or seeds. The plastic holds moisture in, helps plants grow faster and eliminates weeds. It's neater, too—you don't sink in the mud when the ground's wet.  *—Dlores DeWitt*
*Colorado Springs, Colorado*

**If you have** mini-blinds that need to be shortened, save the extra slats. I cut them in pieces and use them to mark rows of seeds.
*—Helen Sanders*
*West Union, South Carolina*

**To strengthen** seedlings and get them accustomed to the wind, place them in front of a fan. First I water my seedlings well. Then I place them about 12 to 24 inches from an oscillating fan running at a very low speed for a half-hour each day.
*—Monica Hutson*
*Byron, Minnesota*

**Add a pinch** of Epsom salts to the hole when planting bulbs. It helps get the bulbs started and keeps squirrels and moles from digging them up. *—Joan Eiffes*
*Lindstrom, Minnesota*

**The first year** I started seeds in my basement, it was too cold for the tomatoes to sprout. So the next year, I put the seeds in 4-inch pots, then put those in larger pots. I covered the big pots with clear plastic lids and set them under a lamp. The seeds sprouted quickly.
*—Irene Jones, Chardon, Ohio*

**I plant tomato seeds** directly in the garden. They develop good roots and produce ripe fruits within 1 week of the plants that I buy and set out. *—Alice Parrish*
*Wray, Colorado*

**When starting** seedlings indoors, I always put a thin layer of sifted sphagnum moss over the soil surface. To sift sphagnum moss, just rub it through a sieve into a container. *—Nancy Pedersen*
*Center City, Minnesota*

**I recycle seed trays** from my annuals purchased from a nursery and use them to start annuals from seed the next year.

In the trays, I use a layer of perlite topped with at least 2 inches of potting soil. I soak the soil with warm water and then scatter the seeds on top. Then I cover with a thin layer of

---

## WORDS TO GROW BY

**To get an early start** in spring, I make a cold frame with straw bales and cover it with old storm windows. Just remember to remove the windows on sunny days so the plants don't get too hot. *—Martha Martin*
*Harriston, Ontario*

---

potting soil and top it off with a *very* thin layer of perlite.

I soak seeds well and mist twice a day. When sprouts develop two secondary sets of leaves, they're ready to transplant into pots or my garden. It works great!
*—Vanessa Cadiere*
*Montegut, Louisiana*

**When planting** small seeds, such as lettuce, don't use your hands or a trowel to cover them with soil. Germination will be inhibited if they're planted too deeply. For a lighter touch, I use a paintbrush.
*—Karen Ann Bland*
*Gove, Kansas*

**Save money** by making your own seed-starting mix. Just combine 2 parts peat moss with 1 part vermiculite. *—Jodie Stevenson*
*Export, Pennsylvania*

**11**

**Like many gardeners**, I've lost many seedlings started indoors to damping-off disease. To avoid this, make sure to use started pots cleaned with 1 part bleach to 9 parts water *and* a sterile seed-starter mix.
—*Jan Bowser, St. Charles, Missouri*

**When I pot plants**, I line the bottom of each pot with three sheets of newspaper. This keeps in the soil and water. My plants always look great. —*Ann Ward*
*Naples, Florida*

**When sowing** small seeds, like petunias, I find they often sprout too thickly. Tweezers are perfect for separating the seedlings without damage. With the tweezers, move the thinned plants to new containers and pat down the soil with the blunt end. —*Barbara Dege*
*Hackensack, New Jersey*

**I use a soil mixture** of equal parts sand, peat moss and homemade compost heated to 160°. Any higher temperature for the compost will de-

---

### HOW TO MAKE NEWSPAPER PLANTING CUPS

**I use newspapers** to make biodegradable planting cups for transplanting seedlings. Cut four thicknesses of newspaper into a 7-inch square, fold in thirds, then turn and fold again to make a 9-square fold. Angle-fold each corner on one side and staple. Repeat on the opposite side.

When seedlings are ready to transplant, plant the entire cup. The seedlings' roots won't be disturbed, and the containers will break down on their own. —*Patricia Murray*
*Niles, Ohio*

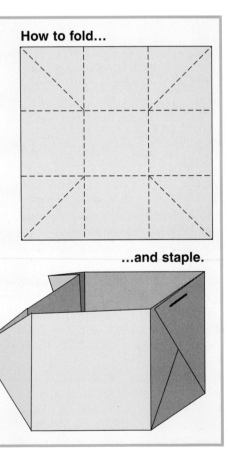

How to fold...

...and staple.

stroy helpful organisms that fight fungus. —*Valerie Evanson*
*Phoenixville, Pennsylvania*

**Dahlia seeds** can be started in yogurt cups with clear lids. Cut a slit in the bottom for drainage, fill with soil to within 1/2 inch of the top, water and put on the lid. Let them sit until they sprout, then remove the lid. When the seedlings form true leaves, they can be transferred to individual pots. —*Irene Jones*
*Chardon, Ohio*

**In early spring**, we punch holes in the bottom of a large can and use it to sprinkle hardwood ashes over the snow in the garden. The snow melts quickly and the earth dries out faster, enabling us to plant earlier. The potash in the ashes is good for the soil, too. (Use sparingly in alkaline soil.) —*Gerri Kurec*
*Cambridge, Ontario*

**When I run** out of space for seedlings on the basement shelf, which is under lights, I start them in an old aquarium. —*Irene Jones*
*Chardon, Ohio*

**We make a** temporary "greenhouse" by putting a picnic table under the A-frame of a lawn swing and covering the frame with a sheet of clear plastic. The sides are held shut with large clothespins. Bricks and blocks weigh down the plastic outside. We also loop ropes over the top of the swing to hold hanging baskets. —*Val and Alma Gingerich*
*Summerfield, Ohio*

**Use an extra** calendar—or an old calendar—to remind yourself when to do various garden chores. Each time you come by new planting or care instructions, write the information under the appropriate dates. For example, I have "prune grapes"

written on Feb. 22, "repot and fertilize poinsettia" written on May 1 and "plant spring bulbs" written on Oct. 15. It doesn't matter what year the calendar is. This just lets me know the time of the year each job should be done.

After several years of adding information, my calendar is fairly complete, and I can tell at a glance what chores need to be done each month. My yard has never looked better! —*Shirley Salyers*
*Columbus, Ohio*

**Winter aconite** is one of the first flowers to bloom in our area—usually in March, sometimes even as early as February. It does best in semi-shade and grows easily from seed. I got excellent results just by dropping the seed on beds of moss around the yard. —*Ellen Pearson*
*Crofton, Maryland*

13

**Before planting** my garden, I let my chickens go through it. They find many insects and larvae that have wintered over.
—*Leo Bexten*
*Ottawa Lake, Michigan*

paper. Over time, the newspaper and cardboard break down and improve the soil. —*Barbara Bishoff*
*Roscommon, Michigan*

**Since it is difficult** to make straight rows, I drive 1-foot stakes at the end of each row and tie a string between them. I use the string as a guideline. —*Mary Schmidt*
*Hawarden, Iowa*

**For a few days** after I plant my bedding plants, I use clay pots to protect them from heat. I cover each plant with a pot during the hottest part of the day.
—*Mrs. Robert Unruh*
*Moundridge, Kansas*

**To make it easier** for seeds to push up through my heavy clay soil, I make small trenches in my garden with a triangle-shaped hoe. I fill each trench with equal parts cactus sand (a product used for planting cactus) and seed-starting mix, then plant the seeds.

If the seeds need darkness to germinate, I cover them with a thin layer of grass clippings (not from lawns with invasive grasses or recently treated with weed killers). Once the seedlings are up and going, they'll root well in the clay.
—*Nancy Pedersen*
*Center City, Minnesota*

**Take asparagus fern** into the house during winter. It may turn yellow and drop needles. But in spring when there's no danger of frost, you can split up the roots and plant it outside. Before long, the clumps will grow to surpass a small nursery plant. —*Nancy Shavlik*
*Bartlett, Nebraska*

**Use a turkey** baster to water plants you have started from seeds indoors. It prevents you from overwatering or flattening the tender plants.
—*Valerie Evanson*
*Phoenixville, Pennsylvania*

**Place layers** of newspaper and flattened cardboard boxes instead of expensive landscaping cloth in your gardens. I put the newspaper and cardboard right over the weeds, soak them well to hold them in place and cover with wood chips. This combination smothers the weeds and the

**A very fine mist** works wonders to revive badly wilted plants, especially in hot weather. Plants that seem almost dead often can be revived with a couple of hours of fine spray, whereas a heavy spray might kill them. This reduces losses when transplanting small seedlings, too. (Mist nozzles that attach to garden hoses are available at most nurseries and garden centers.) —*Dean Gibby Willits, California*

**My daughter**, Diana Stephens, has a no-till garden that's virtually maintenance-free. In early spring, she kills existing weeds with Roundup herbicide. (Other total vegetation killers that *don't last in the soil* will work, too. Read and follow all label directions.)

Two weeks later, after the soil warms, she plants the bed and marks rows with electric fence posts. With a heavy mulch of weathered straw or hay between rows, the few weeds that make it through to daylight can be pulled out easily.

Diana also plants tomatoes much earlier than is normally safe in our area by heavily mulching them and then enclosing them in a "fort" of straw bales. If frost threatens, Diana covers the plants with buckets. On windy spring days, the plants tucked in the fort are protected as they collect sunshine and grow.
—*Joyce Vannice, Hannibal, Missouri*

**I start tomato seeds** under shop lights in early April. When they have four leaves, I transplant them into Styrofoam cups. When the weather settles, I set them outside during the day to harden them off. Then I plant the seedlings when danger of frost is past.
—*Mrs. Roy Starner, Niles, Ohio*

**Use a utility knife** to remove the bottoms of empty 2-liter plastic soft drink bottles. Discard the bottoms and use the remaining portions to cover tender seedlings on cool spring nights. —*Louretta Hicks East Freedom, Pennsylvania*

**I cut off the tops** of 2-liter plastic soft drink bottles to use to protect my seedlings. But I want to recycle the clear bottoms of the bottles, too. So I use them as saucers for my clay pots. They work quite well and protect surfaces from spills when I've overwatered.
—*Shirley Hansen Waldhof, Ontario*

**When I start seeds** indoors, I cover the containers with disposable shower caps at night to keep the soil moist. The cap's elastic ensures that it fits any shape container.
—*Phil Kozol Glendale Heights, Illinois*

**When planting** morning glory seeds or other hard-shelled seeds, soak them in water for 24 hours. Then place them on a damp paper towel and cover them with another paper towel. Once the seeds sprout, carefully remove them from the towels and plant them. Seedlings should be popping out of the soil in a few days.          —*Virginia Petersen*
*Clarendon, Pennsylvania*

**We start our seeds** in plastic soft drink bottles. Cut off the hard bottoms or the lower 3 inches of the bottles if they do not have hard bottoms. Then fill this portion with good potting soil, plant seeds and water. Replace the top and tape in place. Be sure to leave the bottle cap off. You now have a mini-greenhouse!

---

### *Tip from Our "Landlady"*

**Paper egg cartons** *work well for starting seeds. Cut the top off and place it under the egg compartments. Then add seed starting mix and your seeds. When watered, the paper carton holds moisture for a long time and adds support for handling. Break each section apart when transplanting. You can plant the biodegradable carton with the seedling to reduce transplanting shock.*
—*Gail Russell*
*Reiman Publications*

---

The seeds germinate and grow rapidly when placed in a window, but don't forget to vent on warm sunny days to prevent heat buildup. Water sparingly through the open top when all condensation has evaporated.

When plants are ready to set outdoors, remove the top part of the bottle and lift them out.

You can recycle the bottle tops further by cutting away the narrow neck portion. Then push the remaining sleeve into the soil around fragile plants to protect them.
—*Sandy Brooks*
*Aberdeen, Maryland*

**Before I sow fine seeds**, such as wildflower seeds, I mix them with some colored gelatin powder. It helps spread the seeds evenly and it's easy to see where I've sown them. And who knows? It might even nourish the seedlings as they begin to grow.
—*Angela Griffin Hatchett*
*Altoona, Alabama*

**People in the Northeast** often add lime to their acidic garden soil in spring, letting the rain wash it in. I hadn't done this for several seasons, so I mixed 1/2 teaspoon powdered lime per gallon of water when it was time to transplant my tomatoes. It was sunny and in the 80s when I transplanted the tomatoes, so I expected them to wilt. But after watering them with the lime solution, they didn't wilt at all! Now I use this on all my spring transplants. Horticultural lime works best, but

I've used regular lime, too. (Be sure to have your soil tested before adding lime.) *—Carol Boileau Jewett City, Connecticut*

After my plants have sprouted in spring, I lay two thicknesses of newspaper between the plants and rows and then top them with straw. This controls the weeds, keeps the garden moist and frees me for other activities. By fall, the newspapers have broken down.

*—Marilyn Kaufman, Sigel, Illinois*

---

To give tomatoes an early start in our notoriously cold area, we plant tomato seeds indoors in peat pots on April 1.

For each plant, we prepare a 1/2-gallon, wax-coated milk carton. Completely open the carton and slice the corners halfway down. Fold down the flaps you created and secure them with rubber bands.

When plants have two or three leaf pairs, move them to these cartons. Remove all but the top pair of leaves and cover the stem with potting soil. The stem sends out roots where the leaves used to be.

When plants again have several pairs of leaves, remove the rubber bands, straighten the flaps and tape them back in place. (Clear mailing tape does a good job.) Again, remove the bottom leaves, leaving one pair at the top. Fill with soil, covering the stem. Return plants to a sunny spot until they're ready to set outdoors.

This method reduces stress on our tomatoes and enables us to set out strong plants right after Memorial Day, even though we still get minor frosts.

*—Warren Frye and Judith Korman De Lancey, New York*

**Milk Carton Plant Starters**

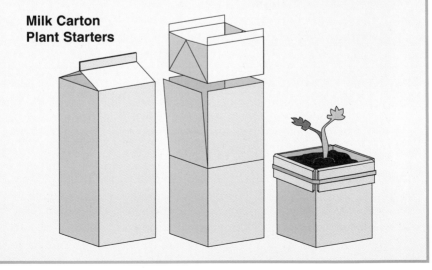

**Cut up mesh bags** that hold grapefruit, oranges or onions and use them to line seed trays before adding planting medium. When annual plants reach transplant size, just lift out the mesh and transplant the whole thing. There's no harm done to the roots of annuals, which will grow through the mesh.

*—Beatrice Maurer*
*Penn Hills, Pennsylvania*

**Use cardboard** soft drink or beer trays and plastic soft drink trays to start your seeds in spring. Plant your seeds in the cardboard flats, which grocery stores are happy to give away. Set the flats in the plastic trays that hold 16-ounce plastic soda bottles. The trays are usually available for the deposit, which is $2 in my area. It sure saves me money.

*—Dotty Reel, Cabool, Missouri*

**To easily start watermelons** and cantaloupes, put seeds between wet paper towels, slip into a zip-top plastic bag and put them in a warm place. After several days, check for sprouts. Once you have 1/2- to 1-inch sprouts, plant them outside. I start with five or six per hill, then thin to the strongest three sprouts. If the weather is still cool, cover the hills with domed hot houses.

*—Mrs. Christ Stoltzfus*
*Leola, Pennsylvania*

**To make my gardens** easier to handle in spring, I start the previous fall by clearing them of old plants and weeds.

In spring, I just have to till the soil. (If the area is small, I just use a spade to turn it over.) Then I use a hoe to make a trench 3 to 4 inches deep. I fill the trench with composted manure, cover the compost with the soil I removed from the trench and plant my seeds.

If the seeds are difficult to germinate (like dill and cucumber seeds), I plant them right in the compost and then cover them. Germination is nearly 100%.

*—Norma Dembraski*
*Bruce Crossing, Michigan*

**Foam drinking cups** make ideal pots for starting seedlings. They are inexpensive, especially if recycled, and are available in a range of sizes. Just punch a few drainage holes in the bottoms of the cups

---

## WORDS TO GROW BY

**Label everything** you plant. Then you will have no question what is coming up in the garden. Also, place the markers deep enough so they will not be lost or broken off. Here's a few more tips: Soak beans overnight before planting and plant a row of sunflowers to attract colorful birds. *—Shirley Van Vleet, Higgins Lake, Michigan*

and write plant names on the sides. At planting time, seedlings slip out so easily that I'm able to use the cups many times before discarding them.                              —*Barbara Hunt*
*Jonesborough, Tennessee*

**Metal juice cans** and plastic soft drink bottles make fine "mini-green-houses" for tomatoes, peppers and eggplants.

I remove the ends from the cans, sink them halfway into the ground and position a plant in the middle. Then I cut the bottoms off the plastic bottles, punch a few small holes around the necks and slip them over the cans and plants.

Since I've started doing this, we've had several spring sleet storms, and my plants weren't damaged. Sometimes I even plant seeds using this method.

By the time the plants outgrow the bottles, the danger of frost usually has passed. After removing the bottles, I mix fertilizer with water and pour it into the can, so the water goes directly to the roots. This makes it easy to water and fertilize at the same time.

—*Patricia Moore*
*Little Rock, Arkansas*

**Create a simple shelf** to provide extra windowsill space when starting seeds indoors in spring.

Use 12-inch wood shelving cut to fit the width of the sill. Use "C"-clamps to secure the front ends of the extensions to the sills.

To create a back support leg, cut a scrap piece of two-by-four to the appropriate length and secure it to the extension with wood screws. Once the extensions are made, they only take a minute or so to set up and take down at the beginning or after each growing season.

—*Cornelius Hogenbirk*
*Waretown, New Jersey*

**Here's an easy way** to help identify what type of soil you have. Place a cup of garden dirt into a clear quart jar and fill the jar with water. Shake the soil and water until it is well mixed. Then let it settle for 24 hours.

The elements in the soil will separate into layers. The layer with the heaviest particles—sand—will be on the bottom, followed by layers of silt and clay.

You should be able to estimate the amount of sand, silt and clay in your soil by the thickness of each layer.

—*Angela Griffin Hatchett*
*Altoona, Alabama*

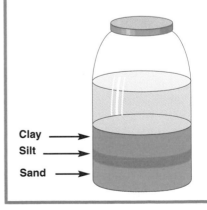

Clay ⟶
Silt ⟶
Sand ⟶

**An old** bacon press that I found at a flea market helps me plant tiny seeds each spring.

After planting the seeds, I cover them with a small amount of soil. Then I use the bacon press to tap them down so they don't wash away. I've done this for several years, and I don't think I've lost a seed yet. —*Cookie Bush*
*Pasadena, Maryland*

---

### Tip from Our "Landlady"

**Cotton balls** *from medicine bottles can be used on top of seed trays to help retain moisture. Remove the cotton when the seeds start sprouting.* —*Gail Russell*
*Reiman Publications*

---

**Don't throw away** extra seedlings after planting what you need. Plant a few between your regular plants in case you need replacements. Then donate the remaining ones to a day-care center or preschool class. Youngsters love to learn about plants, especially if they get to care for their very own.

—*Margaret Shauers*
*Great Bend, Kansas*

**To prevent your seedlings** from suffering transplant shock, use this method to start seeds.

Fill 2-1/4-diameter peat pots with hanging basket mix rather than potting soil. (The hanging basket mix contains perlite and water-holding crystals, which retain moisture and allow the roots to breathe better.)

Use very warm water to wet the mix thoroughly, then plant one seed in each pot.

To keep the peat pots from warping, place them in Styrofoam cups that have drainage holes and have been trimmed to the height of the peat pot. The cups can be used again and again each year.

Put the cups in a tray and cover the tray with plastic wrap. Keep in a warm place until the seeds germinate. After they sprout, remove the plastic and place the cups under grow lights.

When it's time to move the seedlings outside, plant the whole peat pot. Be very careful to completely cover it with soil. This will keep it from drying out. —*Charles Dismer*
*Rock Island, Illinois*

**Carrot seeds** need constant moisture to germinate. So I cover the bed with burlap after the seeds are planted and then keep the burlap damp.

Besides keeping moisture in the soil, the burlap allows the ground to breathe. The seeds should germinate in 5 to 7 days. As soon as they sprout, remove the burlap.

—*Eugene Sommers*
*Hartville, Ohio*

**A "seed board" helps** me plant seeds at the correct depth. On a decking board, I painted the depths at which various seeds should be planted, from 1/4 inch up to 2-1/2 inches.

I use the edge of the board to

## WORDS TO GROW BY

**When transplanting** flowers and vegetables, water them well and then place a roomy clay flowerpot over each plant. Make sure the pots have openings on the top or sides for ventilation. Keep them on the plants for 2 or 3 days. Don't forget to keep the plants moist. This will give them a great start after transplanting.
—*Bertha Beatty*
*Grafton, Ontario*

press down the soil to the desired depth. Then I just add the seeds and cover them with soil.
—*Alice Falkenstein*
*Wilton, North Dakota*

**In spring**, when you have finished planting the flowers you purchased from the nursery, save the plastic plant markers. Those that feature photos of the plants make neat colorful book marks. —*Alice Turner*
*Payson, Arizona*

**When planting** tiny seeds, like carrots or lettuce, mix them with a handful of white sand. Then when you spread the seed-sand mixture, you'll be able to see how thickly and consistently you're planting your rows. —*Eugene Sommers*
*Hartville, Ohio*

**When planting** seed rows, I plant a few onions on the ends so I can tell where the rows of slow germinating seeds are. By the time the onions are ready to pull, the seeds will have sprouted. —*Della Rebbe*
*Fremont, Nebraska*

**Large metal cans** with both ends removed, such as 1-gallon coffee cans, work well when setting out tomato plants. Place a can around each plant and push it about 2 inches into the soil. This makes it easier to water the tomatoes and helps keep cutworms at bay.
—*Mrs. Robert Unruh*
*Moundridge, Kansas*

**With our short growing** season in this part of Canada, sweet peas need an early start. So I fill empty toilet paper tubes with soil to start the plants indoors. When it's time to transplant them outdoors, I just pop the containers into the ground.
—*Anna Heinrichs*
*Altona, Manitoba*

**Before planting seeds** and annuals each spring, I use a garden spade to incorporate the winter debris (such as leaves, stalks and last fall's mulch) into the soil. This adds organic matter to the soil and helps keep it loose.

After I've planted, I add a fresh layer of mulch to my beds, which keeps moisture in and protects plants from any cool nights. —*Connie Moore*
*Medway, Ohio*

**In spring,** I keep my plant starts and nursery purchases outside on a large snowmobile trailer. It holds 100 flats and can be wheeled in and out of the garage. If the wind picks up, I can easily move all the plants inside in a minute.
—*Stan Fitz*
*Rockford, Iowa*

**Place thoroughly** dried seeds collected from your flower and vegetable gardens in plastic bags. Label, seal and store them in the refrigerator. Come spring, you'll be all set for planting.
—*Elsie Kolberg*
*St. Joseph, Michigan*

**Last spring,** frost warnings came late in the season after I had hung my heavy flower-filled baskets outside.

Usually my farmer-husband, Gary, lends me a hand on nights like this, but he was busy out in the fields, and I couldn't take the baskets down by myself.

So I borrowed some of his oversized sweatshirts and jackets to cover the baskets. They had a spooky appearance in the morning, but they certainly helped save my flowers from the frost.
—*Sue Van Gelderen*
*Walnut Grove, Minnesota*

**Here's an easy way** to increase your success when transplanting seedlings. Carry a small squeeze bottle (like the kind liquid dish soap comes in) and a bucket of water so you can refill it.

Squirt the spot where you want to plant a seedling and use a grape-fruit spoon with a serrated edge to dig a hole. After your seedlings are in, squirt the area once more.

The plants won't even know they've been transplanted. It even works well with the most delicate seedlings.
—*Janeen Jackson*
*Roundup, Montana*

**I use the plastic** ditch liner my husband uses for irrigating crops to protect my garden plants. I anchor it at one end of my flowers and keep it rolled up. When bad weather is brewing, all I have to do is go out, unroll the plastic to the other end of the row and anchor it.
—*Mrs. Marvin Kuper*
*Dalhart, Texas*

**During spring gardening,** when the soil starts to dry, I put one of my small boys in his wagon and pull him up and down the garden so the wheels can mark the rows for planting. It's a fun way for me and the boys to get straight rows that are a good distance apart.
—*Lois Noby*
*Great Falls, Montana*

# CHAPTER TWO

# BIGGER, BETTER BLOOMS

SOMETIMES it's the little things that make a difference. That's the case when it comes to producing blooms that will bring color to your gardens throughout the entire growing season.

You'll be surprised at some of these ideas —from giving your plants their morning coffee to "pinching" chrysanthemums for more color.

So read on…this advice from "backyard experts" will keep your place packed with color up until the first frost.

**The secret** to compact beautiful chrysanthemums is to pinch back or trim about half of the plant's new growth. Repeat this until about the first week of July. And be sure to water and fertilize properly.

—*Mrs. Leroy Martin*
*Hagerstown, Maryland*

**Our garden** is next to several large trees, and our flowers never seemed to get enough water—until we started using Soil Moist water-retaining crystals.

We just poke holes in the ground around each plant, drop in a few granules and presto! Our plants get a good drink before the tree roots soak up all the water. Now we work the granules into the soil whenever we plant annuals and shrubs.

—*Rogene Teicheira*
*Concord, California*

**When your Easter lily** is finished blooming, don't throw it out. Let it dry, cut off the old foliage and plant it in a partly sunny spot in the garden. It will grow and bloom again.

—*Eileen Crowley*
*Prairie du Chien, Wisconsin*

**To avoid** the hassles of planting and lifting tuberous begonias, I put them in pots. They can be sunk into the ground or set on top of the soil.

In fall, just before frost, take the pots inside and place in a cool room over winter. I begin watering again in spring as I see signs of life. When the danger of frost has passed, I set them outside again and fertilize weekly throughout the growing season. —*June Hadland*
*Chehalis, Washington*

**To make coleus plants** bigger and bushier, pinch off the flowers when they start to spike. If you don't do this, the plant will grow tall rather than spread out.

—*Naydene Cook, Pisgah, Alabama*

**Sometimes when** naturalizing an area with spring-blooming bulbs, like daffodils and crocuses, you'll find a spot where a plant is missing. Mark it by simply pressing a small tuna can (upside down with the bottom intact) into the soil. This kills the grass underneath and reminds you to plant another bulb to fill the space in fall.

—*Muriel Miller, Sylvia, Kansas*

## WORDS TO GROW BY

**When gathering seeds**, always take them from the largest healthiest blooms. Leave the flower on the plant until it is completely faded and the seed head is dry. Then remove the head and place it on a paper plate to dry. Shake out the seeds and store them in a cool dry place.

—*Lois Wark, Reno, Nevada*

**To keep** a garden in bloom for a long time, alternate your rows with flowers that bloom at different times. One good combination is dahlias, gladiolus and zinnias.
—*Liz McCain, Florence, Oregon*

**When large** sunflowers reseed, they produce much smaller blossoms. I like using the smaller heads as cut flowers. The flowers last a week to 10 days. —*Barbara Eddy Rio Rancho, New Mexico*

**To start** a new plant, I take a cutting no more than 8 inches long, pull off the bottom leaves, dip the end in rooting compound and place in a pot of well-drained damp soil. I put the pot in a shaded area and keep it moist. In about a month, I have a nice new plant. —*Ann Ward Naples, Florida*

**I use plastic** ice cream buckets to start seeds. Cut drainage holes in the bottom of the bucket, fill it about 1/3 full of seed starting mix and plant the seeds. Then water and snap the lid back on. Place the bucket in a warm spot. The plastic diffuses the light nicely. In about 10 days, you'll have plants ready for transplanting.
—*B. Volz Jr., Dexter, Missouri*

**A nursery** worker told me to plant my cleome and cosmos at least 8 inches deep. That way the crowns of the plants were at least 6 inches underground. Both plants bushed out and were much larger and sturdier, standing up to wind and rain without staking. They produced more blooms than usual, too.
—*Mollie Hart, Woodstock, Ontario*

**I'd like to recommend** fabulous Purple Wave petunias. They grow in 15 window boxes attached to the deck of our lakefront home. They're so beautiful that many boaters slow down and soak in their beauty as they cruise by.

The plants cascade on their own without being pinched back. They also work well in hanging baskets. They can be purchased as seeds or plants. —*Donna McCarthy Gravois Mills, Missouri*

**I remove** spent blooms on most flowering plants. This strengthens them and produces more blooms.

Some flowers, like chrysanthemums, benefit from being cut back early in spring so they don't get leggy and fall over later. They'll bloom a bit later, but the plants will be bushier and stronger.
—*Azalea Wright Forest Lake, Minnesota*

**Try planting gladiolus** in narrow spaces. They look great in the 2-foot area between our alley and fence.

I attach fishing line to the fence. This helps hold the flowers up as they get tall.
—*Paul Peterson Redding, California*

**Save money** by purchasing petunias late in spring. The flats I buy are half price because the plants are tall and straggly. Before planting, I loosen the roots and cut the plants back, taking off most of the blooms. The petunias bounce back better than ever.
—*Mrs. Dwight Pippenger*
*Walkerton, Indiana*

**Daylilies** not only fill your yard with dazzling colors, but attract nectar-feeding creatures like hummingbirds, orioles and butterflies.
—*Marlene Condon*
*Crozet, Virginia*

**My mother** has been growing crested cockscomb (*celosia*) for 25 years. They grow beautifully in full sun and become tall plants with gorgeous red blooms. Here's how she does it.

She puts the seeds in a pepper shaker and distributes them over an area that has been well-worked with composted cow manure. After raking lightly, she sprinkles the area with water and continues to keep the soil moist. The young plants resemble beet sprouts and are slightly red under the leaves.

Mom begins thinning as the sprouts develop, keeping the heartiest plants about a foot apart. She also keeps an eye out for squash bugs, which love the cockscomb seeds.
—*Lucille Stier*
*Redding, California*

**When I want** to press some pretty flowers for cards, I put them between facial tissues and press them in the pages of an old telephone book.
—*Monica Bengston*
*Independence, Iowa*

**When I** forced hyacinths to bloom in winter, the buds sometimes didn't rise much above the bulb. I solved this problem by wrapping the pot in an 8-inch tall tube made from a paper grocery bag. This keeps the buds "reaching" for the light. When they're the right height, I remove the bag and put the pot in good light.
—*Becky Olson*
*Arden Hills, Minnesota*

**My geraniums** grew spectacularly when fed the leftover coffee from my mug. I just dumped the last few drops in the planter every day and was rewarded with beautiful foliage and prolific healthy blooms.
—*Sharon Jensen*
*Dubuque, Iowa*

**If you're** having trouble finding the botanical name of a certain plant, try visiting a botanical garden. They usually have at least one variety of most plants or someone who can help you. *—Julie Mira Warner Chadron, Nebraska*

**I soak** potato peelings in water, then water my pot-grown gerani-ums.  *—June Schnader New Holland, Pennsylvania*

**I planted my border** only once and never had to do it again! That's because I used flowers that are self-sowing, such as cleome, larkspur, calendula and cosmos. Each year I get many compliments on it. People don't realize how easy it is. *—Bonita Laettner Angola, New York*

**When you trim** your chrysanthemums back in summer, you may be able to enjoy even more flowers later. I plant the tops I've cut off in the soil along our garage wall. Soon I have enough new plants to share with friends and neighbors. *—Martha Miller Auburn Hills, Michigan*

**To keep cut flowers** fresh for weeks, add any clear soda to your vase. (7-Up, Sprite, ginger ale, etc. Diet sodas, however, should not be used.) I fill the container with half soda and half water. I'm amazed at how long the flowers last. *—Diane Gorsek Cleveland, Ohio*

**Poultry manure** is very good for flowers. Just keep it about 5 inches away from the plants' roots. *—G. Kriculi, Chicago, Illinois*

**To keep** your hanging fuchsia basket full of blooms, pinch off the spent flowers. Do this constantly and the plant will bloom all summer. *—Margaret Lindow Suamico, Wisconsin*

**Dust gladiolus** corms and dahlia tubers with sulfur before storing them for winter. (For safety, always label treated bulbs.) I store corms in open trays and tubers in boxes of peat moss and have seldom had any go bad in storage.

*—Joyce Cooksey Braintree, Massachusetts*

**American goldfinches** love to feed on false nettle (*Boehmeria*) seeds. Although this plant doesn't have showy flowers, its pretty green leaves make an interesting backdrop for shorter flowering plants. It grows about 2 feet tall. *—Marlene Condon Crozet, Virginia*

**I save** the water from boiling eggs and use it (cooled, of course) to water my hanging begonia. The plant blooms continuously.
—*June Schnader*
*New Holland, Pennsylvania*

**Rejuvenate** old perennials by dividing them. If the center of the plant is woody and no longer produces flowers, divide it in half. Cut out and discard the center and cut the remaining ring into smaller pieces. Plant some of these pieces in the same spot and soon you'll see new growth. Plant extra pieces in other areas or share them with friends. —*Angela Griffin Hatchett*
*Altoona, Alabama*

**To grow** big bushy flowers, work several inches of old duck manure into your flower beds. We get ours by the pickup load from a local duck farmer. Aged cow or chicken manure works well, too. Then we keep soaker hoses in our beds all summer long so we can water when it doesn't rain. Our beds look great and don't have many weeds.
—*Donna and Larry Martin*
*Goshen, Indiana*

**When cutting** snapdragons for arrangements, pinch off half of the unopened tips. This will give you a compact flower. —*Ellen Gaugler*
*Hoselaw, Alberta*

**Planting flowers** according to their height (tallest in back and shortest in front) helps prevent them from falling over. For example,

plant tall cannas in the rear of the flower bed, then shorter cosmos in front of them, then gladiolus and finally marigolds as border plants.
—*Monica Bengston*
*Independence, Iowa*

**To fertilize** my plants, I use a mix of fish emulsion and sea kelp as a foliage spray every 2 weeks. I have vigorous pest-free plants.
—*Priscilla Fallas*
*Los Altos, California*

**We attract** hummingbirds and butterflies with monarda (bee balm) and red carnations. They also visit my hanging baskets of begonias.
—*Marcia Briggs*
*Pittsburgh, Pennsylvania*

**I plant** sunflowers, zinnias and Mexican sunflowers (*tithonia*) to attract hummingbirds and other beautiful birds. Having plenty of water available for them also helps.
—*Ella Lucas, Roanoke, Virginia*

**Place fresh-cut flowers** in moist florist oasis until you're able to clean and arrange them. This will keep them fresh.
—*Carol Ann Reimir*
*McHenry, Illinois*

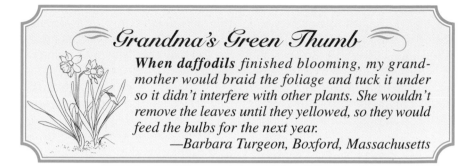

## *Grandma's Green Thumb*

**When daffodils** *finished blooming, my grandmother would braid the foliage and tuck it under so it didn't interfere with other plants. She wouldn't remove the leaves until they yellowed, so they would feed the bulbs for the next year.*
—Barbara Turgeon, Boxford, Massachusetts

**For a real traffic stopper**, put a lot of one type of plant in your yard. It is more attractive when several plants of one kind are grouped together. If using blooming plants, just choose one color.

I also place my blooming borders in front of evergreens. The trees make a nice dark backdrop and the blossom colors seem even more brilliant. —*Alice Dunsdon Glenwood, Iowa*

**When growing** tuberous begonias, I plant them in a potting mix I make myself. I combine half of a bag of potting soil and half of a bag of peat moss. I sometimes add a little diluted fish emulsion as fertilizer. I've even neglected these flowers, and I still get great results.
—*Stacy Nelson Mattituck, New York*

**I save** seeds from impatiens every year. When I set out new impatiens the following spring, I sprinkle the seeds I've saved between the new plants. I have tons of beautiful flowers in bloom all summer.
—*Maria Scocca Cherry Hill, New Jersey*

**Cedar mulch** is the best thing I've done to my flower gardens. I started by spreading it about 2 inches thick and add a little more here and there every spring. I'm weeding less and enjoying my flowers more.
—*Kay Grinsteiner Daggett, Michigan*

**To grow** huge flowers (and lots of veggies), I mix 6 tablespoons Epsom salts and 6 tablespoons Miracle-Gro fertilizer in the hand sprayer attached to my garden hose.
—*Juanita Scalia Enfield, Connecticut*

**To get a great show** from pansies in spring, I plant them in pots and then cut off all the flowers and buds. (I save the blooms for my pressed-flower projects.)

In about 3 to 4 weeks, I have pansies about three times the size of the pot! It works every time and the show lasts about a month.
—*Stacy Nelson Mattituck, New York*

**For sunflowers,** I prepare a shallow hole 12 inches in diameter and plant 6 seeds around it. At the back of the hole, I drive in a tomato stake or broom handle. When the sunflowers get tall, I tie them to the stake. This also works for corn if you don't have lots of room.
—*Joan Rousseau*
*Dudley, Massachusetts*

**I plant** zinnia seed (mostly red) along my garden path every year. Yellow finches come, sometimes by the dozen, to clean the seeds out of the spent flowers. What a splash of color!       —*Dorene Grebing*
*Frohna, Missouri*

**Pansies can** be planted in early spring when temperatures are cool in New England. Just wait until frost leaves the ground. They'll even survive an early-spring snow.
—*Beverly Watson*
*West Hartford, Connecticut*

**The summer** blooming clematis growing on our garage wall is at least 50 years old. In winter, I cut the plant down to about 10 inches and mound it with soil.     —*G. Kriculi*
*Chicago, Illinois*

**When sowing** wildflower seeds, combine 1 or 2 pounds of soil with a scant handful of seeds in a container. Mix well, then cast the mixture around the planting area. You get better-spaced plants, and they'll be fuller because they're not crowded.       —*Gloria Stokes*
*Minden, Nevada*

**I work used coffee** grounds into the soil around my acid-loving plants, such as azaleas. This keeps the soil moist and loose, which helps the shrubs thrive.
—*Vestal Dean Baily*
*Lowell, Indiana*

**To save flower seeds,** use string or a rubber band to secure a paper bag around the seed pods. When the pods are dry, cut the stem and bring the bags indoors. Then it's easy to shake the seeds out of the bag and into an airtight container for storage.       —*Florence Reindl*
*Fairless Hills, Pennsylvania*

**Many people** believe that if you grow cactus, you never have any color in your garden. You may have to wait a little while for it, but the color can be spectacular in our warm climate.

The trick is giving cactus a thorough soaking once a week and liquid fertilizer once each month, until October. Our cactus usually bloom five or six times a season.
—*Helen Penney*
*Hemet, California*

**When the** first buds show on zinnias, roses or marigolds, pinch them off. You'll soon have a bushy plant with more blooms. Keep old blooms picked off, too.    —*Ruth Croson*
*Chattanooga, Tennessee*

**I put my geraniums** in the basement before the first frost. They get filtered sunlight and are watered every 4 to 6 weeks. In early spring, I set them in a protected area next to the house, cut back all dead leaves and stems, then fertilize and water. In a few weeks, the plants are full and budding. One purple geranium has been blooming for 4 years.
—*Tina Jacobs*
*Wantage, New Jersey*

**I mix two varieties** of nasturtium seed—Whirlybird Blend and Alaska—before planting. This provides an interesting bed with different heights and variegated foliage. It would be especially pretty on a slope.    —*Alice Parrish*
*Wray, Colorado*

**After the** first frost in my area, I give my amaryllis 8 weeks of rest in a cool (not cold) dark place so it will be ready to bloom about Christmastime.    —*Louise Theriault*
*Waltham, Massachusetts*

**Whenever you** deadhead your plants, throw the flower heads back into the garden. You'll get free flowers the following spring!

I get free petunias, marigolds, snapdragons, alyssum, nicotiana, cosmos, hollyhocks, poppies and more. If you don't like where the new flowers come up, just move them or weed them out.

You can also do this by waiting until spring to clean out your flower beds. (Be sure to remove diseased and insect-damaged plants in fall.) Shake the dead plants well so the seeds fall and sow themselves. My alyssum comes back by the dozens —and it's an annual!    —*Peg Lair*
*Kenyon Minnesota*

**For bushier perennials** with more flowers, pinch out the growing tips of each stem. On the other hand, for fewer but larger prize-winning blooms on your perennials, pinch out the side buds and leave the central bud in each cluster.
—*Angela Griffin Hatchett*
*Altoona, Alabama*

**My mother** and grandmother taught me to save money on annuals by taking "slips" of plants in fall. Make cuttings from healthy plants. Root the cuttings in water or a well-drained potting mix, then grow in a sunny window all winter. They'll be ready to set out in spring.
—*Sharon Bradshaw*
*Richmond, Missouri*

**For the freshest** cut flowers, pick blooms early in the day while it's cool. Carry a container of lukewarm water and place the stems in the water as soon as they're cut.
—*Angela Griffin Hatchett*
*Altoona, Alabama*

**Here's a hint** for keeping a new perennial bed colorful all summer long—interplant it with colorful annuals. The annuals will fill in the bare spots until your perennials get established. If your perennial garden is in its second or third year, plant the annuals in pots and add them wherever you'd like color.
—*Marie Blahut*
*Yorkton, Saskatchewan*

**Insert geranium cuttings** into a wet block of florist oasis. Keep the oasis moist, but do not let it stand in water. In a short time, you'll see white roots coming through the block. It's not necessary to remove the oasis when transplanting the cuttings. But be sure to completely cover the oasis with soil. This method should work for other plants, too.
—*Eileen Buth*
*Pelican Rapids, Minnesota*

**When I root** plant cuttings in a glass bottle or jar, I put some charcoal used for aquarium filters in the bottom of the container, then add water. I think this helps keep the water clean.
—*John Clayton Jr.*
*Wilmington, North Carolina*

**Cut back** petunias in mid-July to keep them short and bushy. This also helps them bloom longer.
—*Mary Stager*
*Silver Bay, Minnesota*

**Parsley** makes a beautiful border around a flower garden. It's a convenient, practical way to have fresh parsley on hand for cooking and garnishes. And it is a conversation piece, too. I always get lots of compliments.
—*La Verne Strittholt*
*Fairfield, Ohio*

**To make flowers last** long past their blooming time, press them! I put my garden blooms between sheets of tissue paper and place them in books with a weight on top.

When they're dry, I glue them in pretty designs on heavy paper and frame them. They look lovely hanging on a wall and they make wonderful gifts.
—*Louretta Hicks*
*East Freedom, Pennsylvania*

**When adding** native plants to your landscape, start slowly by planting them as accents in your regular beds.
—*Marsha Melder*
*Shreveport, Louisiana*

**When planting** wildflowers, remember to use plants native to your growing climate. They will thrive in your area. —*Mrs. Jim Hines*
*Tallahassee, Florida*

**Next time** a large tree is toppled by storms in your yard, think of the bright side as we did when a Russian olive tree fell. It left plenty of exposed soil underneath to plant a wildflower garden. It was easy and very pretty. —*Jeanne Carrier*
*North Dartmouth, Massachusetts*

**I'm an iris lover.** Here's how I keep them looking great year after year.

I only use bone meal for fertilizer and pull blooms off as soon as they fade. When all the blooms on a plant are finished, I cut the plant's stalk and remove the leaves as they yellow. By the first week of November, I cut the fanned leaves back.

It's very important to keep your irises clean of old leaves. This helps keep iris borers away.
—*Audrey Blay, Moravia, New York*

**I love to grow** tall zinnias. They look their best when I let them grow about 2 feet tall and then stake them so they don't flop over from strong wind or grow sideways. —*Samuel Mott*
*St. Michaels, Maryland*

**Do not** overfertilize impatiens or they'll produce only leaves. If this happens, just wait. In time, they should start blooming again.
—*Joan Fuchs, Morgan, Minnesota*

**Plant ground cover** such as vinca, thyme, creeping veronica and baby's breath over hardy bulbs. The ground cover keeps weeds from growing in the bed.
—*Joan Fuchs, Morgan, Minnesota*

**I use** my garden pond to help force spring bulbs to bloom. Here's how I do it.

Each fall, I empty my small shallow garden pond. Then I fill it with pots of spring flowering bulbs and pack it full of leaves before covering it with a board.

After the bulbs receive the needed cold treatment, I move the pots indoors to grow and bloom. I extend their indoor blooming period by moving only a few pots in at a time.
—*Jim Kloss*
*Milwaukee, Wisconsin*

**When planting** gladiolus bulbs, tilt them a little. When the plants bloom, they will have less of a tendency to fall over.
—*Monica Bengston*
*Independence, Iowa*

**Sit on** a footstool when you're weeding flower beds. It's a lot easier on the knees. —*Beverly Watson*
*West Hartford, Connecticut*

**Each summer**, I set my amaryllis in a sunny spot outdoors. I remove the pot, but don't disturb the soil. Some continue to bloom, so they must enjoy this "vacation". Before frost, I dig and repot them with new soil and bring them into the house.
—*Alice Parrish, Wray, Colorado*

**Flowers that grow well** from their own seeds include zinnia, marigold, bachelor's button, larkspur, perennial sweet pea, California poppy, cosmos, snapdragon, petunia, morning glory and celosia.
—*John and Eula Henline*
*Mitchell, South Dakota*

**My husband and I** would often drive past a garden of beautiful dahlias. What amused us was that many of the plants were shaded by colorful umbrellas.

One day we stopped to ask Larry Moore about his umbrella garden. To our surprise, he explained that the umbrellas were there to slow down the blooming process by shading the plants from the hot sun. That way they'd be perfect for the county fair.
—*Anna Weizman*
*Dayton, Ohio*

**When planting** a garden bed, use a combination of seeds and bedding plants. Bedding plants quickly produce colorful results, but seeds are more economical—especially for gardeners who plant several beds.
—*Rosemary Weaver*
*Garner, Iowa*

**When you bring in** cut flowers from the garden to make a bouquet in the house, always trim the stems on a slant or angle instead of straight across. This helps the flowers take in water because the stems are not sitting flat on the container's bottom. The flowers stay fresher.
—*Hazel Mallory*
*Vallejo, California*

**My amaryllis plant** has multiplied several times since I received the original bulb. I keep replanting its offshoots in one large pot...now I have a beautiful bouquet of blooms in February.
—*Sue Berke*
*Minneapolis, Minnesota*

**My secret** to thriving annuals is to feed them with liquid fertilizer about every 2 weeks. I feed roses a rose fertilizer about once a month. I continue to fertilize all my flowers through August 1. This system results in beautiful flowers.
—*Dorothy Ruh*
*New Holstein, Wisconsin*

### Tip from Our "Landlady"

*Water sunflowers well. Their roots will then run deep into the soil, giving the plant more support as it grows tall.*
—*Gail Russell*
*Reiman Publications*

# CHAPTER THREE

# SHEDDING LIGHT ON SHADE

DON'T be in the dark just because your backyard is blanketed in shade. There are several ways to add splashes of color even to the shadiest corners.

From plants that thrive without a lot of sun, like hostas and impatiens, to "forever gardens" painted on a garage wall, we're sure you'll find several ways to brighten your landscape.

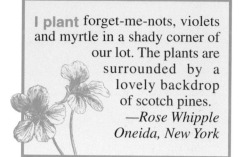

**I plant** forget-me-nots, violets and myrtle in a shady corner of our lot. The plants are surrounded by a lovely backdrop of scotch pines.
—*Rose Whipple*
*Oneida, New York*

**Adding color** to a densely shaded area of my garden was easy and inexpensive. I planted three bleeding hearts, three elephant ear bulbs, two rhododendrons, six lily-of-the-valley, three hostas, three ferns, a dozen violets and a flat of impatiens and caladium.

I spent $10 for the flat, plus $6 for mulch. The remaining plants—all perennials—came from my yard or from neighbors who traded for other plants. —*Joanne Craft-Lane*
*Sumter, South Carolina*

**To add color** in shady areas, try caladiums. We plant several hundred caladium bulbs in our yard each summer.

They require little work—just plenty of shade and moisture. I find that planting most of them in pots makes watering them easier. (When they're planted in beds, the water tends to run off the soil.) They reward us with colorful foliage from late May until late September.
—*Mrs. Douglas Lopp*
*Thomasville, North Carolina*

**Consider making** a winding path through shady areas. A path alone will create interest, giving a woodsy feel. I added shade-loving perennials along my path and a bench for enjoying its solitude.
—*Judy Hoolsema*
*Portage, Michigan*

**I brightened** a shady spot by painting sunflowers and a trellis with pink flowers on the garage wall. I can see it from my kitchen window. It gives me a good chuckle every time the snow flies.
—*Barbara Turgeon*
*Boxford, Massachusetts*

**We surrounded** a shady pond on our lot with plenty of hostas. They grow beautifully in the shade.
—*Linda Kovalchick*
*Spokane, Washington*

**Use wax begonias** in shade gardens. They provide nice leaf contrast and pretty flowers.
—*Jackie Egerton*
*Reisterstown, Maryland*

**When wild violets** invaded my shade garden, I learned that only total vegetation killers (chemicals such as Roundup, Kleenup or Finale, which kill only green plants and *do not* stay in the soil) would get rid of them. But how could I spray them without hurting the nearby flowers? The solution was to cut both ends off a large coffee can and "surround" the violets before spraying.
—*Pamela Phelps*
*Watertown, New York*

**Here are some** of my favorite shade plants—begonias, daylilies, Dutchman's breeches, hydrangeas and bleeding hearts.
*—Anne Thompson*
*Staten Island, New York*

---

## WORDS TO GROW BY

**The best thing** you can put in your garden is your shadow. Spending a lot of time there is the best way I know to fight weeds and pests.
*—Virginia Fitzner*
*Cheney, Washington*

---

**A swing** or bench and pots of shade-loving flowers will add color to a dark area of your yard. Hanging baskets of ferns, fuchsia or ivy are lovely. In summer, move tall indoor plants outside to fill empty spaces with their greenery. *—Jewell Thomas*
*Lenoir City, Tennessee*

**Snow-on-the-mountain** brightens our heavily shaded yard. The white and light-green leaves are attractive against the dark greens and browns of the adjoining woods. It requires no care and fills in beautifully. (It can be aggressive, so plant in plastic pots as suggested by Susan Tyndall on page 87.)
*—Margaret Lindow*
*Suamico, Wisconsin*

**Moss will spread** quickly when a leaf blower is used to keep the area clear of debris. Just take a few patches of moss and transplant them in a shady area. Then blow over it as needed. *—Dolly Tomalinas*
*Perrineville, New Jersey*

**Here's an easy way** to create a rock garden on a shady porch. Poke holes in potting soil bags (add a few for drainage, too) and plant impatiens in them. Then place rocks around the bags. There are no weeds to contend with, and you can garden even on rainy days without getting wet! *—Dorothy Seward*
*Reynolds, Indiana*

**Don't cover** a tree's roots with dirt to add flowers because it can damage the tree. We encircled a silver maple with cinder blocks. Each block was filled with potting soil and four impatiens plants. Before you knew it, the shady spot was full of color, and it wasn't real expensive. Best of all, our tree is still healthy, too. *—Ron and Julie Kula*
*Central City, Nebraska*

**I bring color** to my shady yard by hanging baskets of impatiens.

There are other advantages to these baskets, too. Hummingbirds enjoy impatiens, and the hungry critters that eat the flowers planted in my yard can't reach them.
*—Richard Walters*
*North Myrtle Beach, South Carolina*

**We created** a beautiful display of tuberous begonias by mounting 2- x 12-inch boards on heavy brackets beneath our breezeway windows. We cut holes in the boards to hold clay pots, keeping them secure and off the ground, away from small children and animals.
*—Mary Wylie, Grayling, Michigan*

**Whenever I use** an egg, I drop the shell in a container of water with a lid on it and save it until it's time to water my ferns.

In less than a year, one fern outgrew its pot, then was planted into a larger pot. I had to transplant it again later! I thank my mother-in-law for sharing her "eggshell water tip" with me!
*—Rhonda Zimmerman*
*East Earl, Pennsylvania*

**Thanks** to other gardeners, I've compiled a list of plants that thrive in full and partial shade. (It's best to check seed packets or growing instructions for light requirements and suitability to the winters in your area.)

Besides impatiens, shade plants recommended include: astilbe, bleeding heart, bugbane, caladium, calla lily, coleus, columbine, hardy fern, foxglove, hardy geraniums, hosta, ivy, lily of the valley, pansy, hardy primrose, tuberous begonia, trillium, vinca, Virginia bluebell and wild ginger.
*—Wade Deemer*
*Massillon, Ohio*

**Plant white impatiens** in a shady garden to make it bright and noticeable. The white flowers look nice at night, too.
*—Patricia Ernst*
*Cincinnati, Ohio*

**Ferns and hostas** are wonderful shade plants. However, we've added impatiens for a splash of color to complement these lush green perennials.
*—Kristie Statz*
*Cross Plains, Wisconsin*

**I had a real** garden challenge— finding something to add color under the shady canopy of five large maple trees.

So I tried impatiens. They were perfect and bloomed like crazy.
*—Monica Meulemans*
*Wrightstown, Wisconsin*

---

**Spring bulbs** can be planted in areas that are typically shaded by deciduous trees (ones that lose their leaves in fall). That's because they'll grow and flower before the trees leaf out again.
*—Anne Thompson*
*Staten Island, New York*

## CHAPTER FOUR

# HOLD EVERYTHING!

## (Container Gardening)

FROM CERAMIC POTS to old work boots, container gardening is fun and easy. Plus, it allows you to garden in small spots, casily bring tender plants indoors before winter and add color to areas that need brightening up.

The basics are the same no matter which container you choose. So try some of these suggestions from our readers...who knows, your container garden may even include the kitchen sink!

You won't have to water plants as often if you use water-retaining crystals. They store moisture and slowly release it as the plants need it. When I buy a plant, I mix the crystals into the soil of a larger container and repot the plant. I've had a lot of success with this method.
—*Mary Moore Ritchie*
*Raleigh, North Carolina*

When choosing pots for planting vegetables outdoors, bigger is definitely better. The plants thrive because the soil doesn't dry out as fast.
—*Ellen Gaugler*
*Hoselaw, Alberta*

For raised garden beds, we use old tractor tires. All my husband needed to do was use a carpet knife to cut the bead out of the tires.

With our sandy soil, we can water and fertilize the small areas quickly. We also can sit on the edge of the tire while we weed.

It's a lot easier than building raised beds out of lumber.
—*Bridget Lyons*
*Windom, Minnesota*

I love nooks and crannies. My favorite thing is to add a birdbath, bird feeder, birdhouse and, if the spot is shady, a big pot of impatiens. If it's a sunny area, I'll substitute salvia. The birds, squirrels, hummingbirds and butterflies add a lot of life to those lifeless areas. —*Linda Carter*
*Pearl River, Louisiana*

I maximize space on my balcony garden by not only putting containers on the floor, but also hanging flowerpots from the balcony railing. Trailing plants like Purple Wave petunias and ivy-leaf geraniums provide spectacular cascades from these hanging planters.
—*Barbara Dege*
*Hackensack, New Jersey*

Use a wick of absorbent material (like a cotton or wool rag) in flower pots. I place it through the drain hole and lay it in the drain tray. The wick helps water the container. When the drain tray is empty, you know the soil must be dry, too.
—*Lorraine Massey*
*Hermitage, Tennessee*

I filled an old rowboat halfway with rocks for drainage and topped it with dirt and potting soil. Then I planted moss roses grown from seed. The flowers provide nice blooms from June until frost, and I've had many comments on the unusual container. —*Don Head*
*Abilene, Texas*

**Fill an old wheelbarrow** with potting soil and plants, then place it wherever you need a point of interest or color. In fall, I fill mine with straw, mums and pumpkins.

—*Gay Nicholas*
*Henderson, Texas*

**I like to plant** assorted varieties of sedum in pots. They survive winter in our area and do well even if the containers get dry in summer.

—*Valerie Giesbrecht*
*Othello, Washington*

**Foam "peanuts"** used for packing material work well in the bottom of outdoor pots and containers. They help provide drainage and make the pots much lighter. —*Betty Lee*
*Columbus, Wisconsin*

**In autumn**, when the plants in my flower box are done blooming, I fill it with dried flowers from my garden. This way I can enjoy its beauty all year-round.

—*Victoria Tesch*
*Wausau, Wisconsin*

**To make** a miniature rock garden indoors, you'll need a small pre-scription bottle or a disposable medicine cup and a colored plastic lid. Wedge the container in place on the lid with small pretty pebbles. Add a little piece of driftwood or a larger rock beside it and fill the container with water to display small sprigs of flowers. —*Edna Philagios*
*Denison, Texas*

**No room** for a garden? That doesn't mean you can't have vegetables. We grow ours in containers on the driveway. Our garden includes tomatoes, peppers, green onions, peas and pole beans. We also grow container varieties of zucchini, squash, herbs, leeks, radishes, Swiss chard, spinach, leaf lettuce, strawberries and even a dwarf apple tree.

—*Ellen and Roger Caywood*
*Olympia, Washington*

**Use 5-gallon buckets** inside large ceramic decorator pots that don't have drain holes. Drill holes in the bottoms of the buckets for drainage and place them on top of large rocks or bricks inside the pot.

—*Reis Pond*
*Thousand Oaks, California*

**An old wheelbarrow** hides the septic tank cover in the middle of my new flower bed. We drilled drain holes in the bottom, filled it with potting soil and added bedding plants. It looks nice and can be rolled out of the way when necessary. *—Renate Sprague*
*Artois, California*

**When I work** on potted plants, I put recycled newspapers or freezer wrap under the pots to help with clean-up. *—Monica Bengston*
*Independence, Iowa*

**I turned the old rack** that holds the jars in my canner into a hen-and-chicks planter. All I did was stuff sphagnum moss into and all around the rack, press in soil, add more moss and wrap the entire rack with chicken wire.

I planted several varieties of hen-and-chicks and sat the planter on the ground for a couple of weeks until the plants rooted. Then it was ready to hang. It makes a beautiful circle of color and texture.

In winter, I move the planter to a sheltered part of the yard. It's very hardy and can be hung again in spring.

I had a thick mass of plants the first year. After that, I started harvesting the "chicks" for friends.
*—Jean Atter, Boyd, Wisconsin*

**I combine soil** with sand and compost, then mix in ground eggshells, a little human hair, ground banana peels and pencil shavings. My potted plants stay healthy and happy when planted in this mix.
*—Monica Bengston*
*Independence, Iowa*

**I grow lots** of hot peppers in 1- to 3-gallon pots, depending on the plant's mature size. Chinese Five-Color, Czechoslovakian Black and Brazilian Christmas peppers are decorative as well as tasty. The larger plants also look nice with lobelia or alyssum planted around their bases. *—Sue Gronholz*
*Columbus, Wisconsin*

**One of the best flowers** to use in containers is impatiens. I planted some in a large circular planter. They thrived, growing more than 4 feet tall! *—Dee Jayne*
*Johnston, Iowa*

**We laid cement blocks** with their holes facing up, filled the holes with earth and potting soil and set a plant in each. We watered regularly and fed with Miracle-Gro fertilizer.

**After a trip** to Switzerland, my husband was so impressed with the beautiful window boxes that he built one for hanging flowers on our front porch. In winter, I fill the boxes with sprigs of greenery and silk poinsettias.
*—Darlene Paugstat*
*Georgetown, Kentucky*

There was so much produce we were giving it away. Relatives with a big garden said we harvested more than they did. *—Emily Martin*
*Moultrie, Georgia*

**I've found a good** use for bird feeders that have been destroyed by our area squirrels. I clean them out, fill them with potting soil and plant annuals or hardy ivy. They turn out really nice. *—Margaret Hoffman*
*La Plata, Maryland*

**Don't laugh**—I use bathtubs as raised beds. I plant two rows of string beans in each tub. At picking time, I just drive my electric scooter alongside and harvest.
*—Frances Wood*
*Fort Ann, New York*

**Just about anything** can be recycled into a planter. Line a basket with plastic (but keep it under cover from rain), or fill old cowboy boots with gravel, potting soil and plants. Impatiens and ivy look especially good spilling over the tops of boots. I have a pair beside my front door, and people always comment on them. *—Christine Olson*
*Seiad Valley, California*

**We had to** give up normal gardening when we could no longer kneel to plant or pull weeds. But we missed it! So now we have four patio tomato plants and four pots of green peppers. This year, I tried planting leaf lettuce around the edges of a big pot, with carrots in the middle. Both did very well.
*—Mary Margaret Cosens*
*Mackinaw City, Michigan*

**When some neighbors** gave us an old iron bed they'd found in their barn, I decided it would look great outside, filled with flowers. Impatiens made a beautiful "quilt". It looked so inviting that one day I found my 2-year-old granddaughter sprawled out in the middle of my "flower bed"! *—Ruth Ann Burns*
*Laura, Ohio*

**Save your husband's** worn-out work boots. Plant them with hen-and-chicks or pink-blossomed strawberries. They look darling under a bush, on a corner of the deck, or just filling a bare spot in a flower bed. *—Diana Jones*
*Harrisburg, Oregon*

**A straight-backed** wooden chair without a seat makes a great holder for a flowerpot. Just set it wherever you need a little color in your garden.
—*Gay Nicholas*
*Henderson, Texas*

**When I have** large barrels or pots to fill with soil, I put crushed plastic milk containers or soft drink cans in the bottom. The pots weigh less, the drainage is excellent, and I use less potting soil. —*Linda Chartrant*
*Milan, Ohio*

**For an interesting planter**, fill an old pair of work boots or an old lunch box with soil. Don't forget to provide drain holes.
—*Darlene Wyness*
*Williams Lake, British Columbia*

**Mix 1 tablespoon** Epsom salts in a gallon of water for watering container plants.
—*Therese Barry*
*Metairie, Louisiana*

**My mother's** flower boxes were works of art. She used orange crates and flat wooden grape, peach and cherry boxes discarded by grocers. She nailed small twigs to the sides of the boxes for a rustic look and put them on posts, porches and windowsills.
—*Charles Martin*
*Bartlesville, Oklahoma*

**When my husband** and I moved to the city, we had very little space to continue gardening. We planted cucumbers in containers at each end of the porch and allowed the vines to climb a trellis. The vines were not only decorative and productive, but supplied some welcome shade.
—*Dolores Mitcheltree*
*Las Vegas, Nevada*

**Use a broken piece** of pottery over the drain hole of a flowerpot to keep the potting soil from leaking out. Check to make sure water still drains from the hole.
—*R.G. Dinklocker*
*Minersville, Pennsylvania*

**To create** a decorative rock planter, use a hammer and chisel to form a hollow in a lava rock (don't forget to wear safety glasses). Then fill with garden soil and plant with hardy plants like sedum or hen-and-chicks.
—*Bonita Laettner*
*Angola, New York*

---

### Tip from Our "Landlady"

***To lighten the load*** *in large hanging baskets, use packing peanuts in a mesh onion sack to fill space. Use a soil-less planting mix around the peanuts and plant as usual. This method also works well in half whiskey barrels, large clay pots and in flower boxes.* —*Gail Russell*
*Reiman Publications*

**I move containers** of geraniums into our sunroom in winter. This protection, a little fertilizer and regular watering keeps the flowers blooming all winter. —*Spence Devitt Roswell, New Mexico*

**Place used dryer** sheets in the bottom of flowerpots and planters to keep the soil from falling out. —*Vestal Dean Bailey Lowell, Indiana*

**After cooking** vegetables, pour any leftover water onto your container plants. The nutrients help the plants thrive. —*Therese Barry Metairie, Louisiana*

**Dress up** rusty clothesline poles by wiring a trellis to each post. Work up the soil in front of the trellis or add a planter for morning glories. They reseed themselves and make my wash area look pretty. —*Marie Faubert Pain-Court, Ontario*

**Use an inexpensive** plastic birdbath to add colorful flowers to a shady spot. Make a few holes in the basin for drainage and add potting soil. Then fill with plants, such as impatiens, that do well in shade and spill over the sides. —*Evelyn Iden, Filion, Michigan*

**When planting** pots with annuals in the spring, leave the potting soil down 1 inch or so from the top of the pot and cover with mulch. The mulch helps keep the soil cool and holds in moisture. —*Sally Micheel Indianapolis, Indiana*

**I've always wanted** a deck, but until it's financially possible, I've found a way to make do. I found a perfect shady spot under our maple tree and staked out a patio shape. Then I covered the grass with a thick layer of newspaper and laid 2 inches of cedar mulch on top. I placed a few outdoor chairs, a pop crate for a table and added flowers in window boxes that sit on the ground. We now call this area my patio. —*Marie Faubert Pain-Court, Ontario*

**To save** on potting soil, line a planter with a layer of discarded cuttings or dry leaves. The material keeps the soil from washing out of the drain holes and will decompose by the end of the gardening season. —*Elisabeth Tiessen St. Paul, Minnesota*

**Use a 5-gallon bucket** as planting containers for potatoes. This saves time and space. And they're easy to harvest...just tip the pail over. —*Nin Neil Munhall, Pennsylvania*

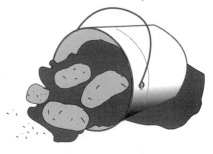

**Flowerpots** around the railing on the porch are easily blown off by strong winds. If you drive a nail about 3 inches long into the top of the railing and slip the drain hole in the bottom of the pot over the nail, you will have no more trouble with the pot falling off. —*Wilma Shauers Beeler, Kansas*

**When arranging** fresh flowers, crisscross the top of the vase or pitcher with clear tape, leaving openings for stems. This makes flower placement a breeze and keeps the blooms from flopping over.
—*Evelyn Sherk Plattsville, Ontario*

**To provide** a sweep of color on our small lot, we use several different types of planters together. Low ones are placed in front with taller planters and hanging baskets rising toward our fence top. This gives the impression that we have acres of flowers spilling beyond our patio fence. —*Joseph and Mary Stemach Eureka, California*

**In regions** where winters aren't too cold, spring-flowering bulbs can be planted in containers and window boxes. —*Marsha Melder Shreveport, Louisiana*

**I saw a clever display** at a florist shop in Westport, Connecticut. It had a wheelbarrow overflowing with flowers. The flowers filled the wheelbarrow and spilled over the side by arranging potted flowers on a small stairway leading to the ground. (A small stepladder would work well, too.) It looked just like a "flower fall"—which happened to be the name of the shop.
—*Shirley Woytach Newtown, Connecticut*

**We set some** of our flowers planted in containers on concrete blocks within our flower gardens. This provides interest at different heights.
—*Justin Schipper Hudsonville, Michigan*

**Pumpkins** make bright autumn planters. I just cut off the tops of the pumpkins, scrape out the seeds and fibers and add pots of chrysanthemums. I also use them as vases for fresh cut flowers. Just add water! —*Edith Gowen, Westbrook, Maine*

**I created a pyramid** of flowers by using end pieces of 8-, 10- and 12-inch PVC pipe. They had been discarded when a friend installed an irrigation system.

I just stacked pieces that were the same diameter to create different heights and slipped in 1-, 2- and 3-gallon black containers (the type you get when buying nursery trees and shrubs) filled with potting mix and annuals. They fit snugly inside the pipe, have holes for drainage and can be easily removed and brought into the garage on cool spring nights. —*Kathie Gilreath Helena, Montana*

# CHAPTER FIVE

# EVERYTHING'S COMING UP ROSES

A ROSE isn't just a rose. For some, it's a trophy of their efforts in the garden. For others, it brings back treasured memories of Grandma and her green thumb.

Here's some advice you'll want to try from our down-to-earth "rose experts". Many painstakingly pamper their garden treasures, while others have found ways to enjoy roses without a lot of work.

There just may be a rosier future for your garden, too.

**Plant garlic** around roses to keep insects away. *—Betty Sullenberger Salt Lake City, Utah*

**To wipe out** black spot on your roses, use the following recipe. Combine 2 tablespoons of baking soda, 1 teaspoon of dishwashing liquid and 1 gallon of water. Spray this solution on roses once a week or when the problem arises. It has saved my roses! *—Stacy Nelson Mattituck, New York*

**To rid** your rosebushes of aphids, cut thin strips of banana peels and hang them from the branches close to the stem. *—Eleanor Peters Port Ludlow, Washington*

**Don't throw away** banana peels. Put them around the bases of your roses and cover them with mulch. Your rosebushes' blooms will be quite a bit larger. *—Winnie Granwehr Sarasota, Florida*

**Don't plant** an expensive rose in a poorly dug hole. It's better to plant a cheap rose in a well-prepared hole.

Dig a hole 1-1/2 feet deep and several feet wide. Remove most of the soil, mix it with peat or another source of humus and return the mixture to the hole. (Roughen the sides of the hole to give the roots a place to grow.)

This is hard work if your subsoil is clay or hardpan. But once the job is done, you won't have to do it again. *—Bill Ott White Lake, Michigan*

**Water roses** regularly in the morning to ward off black spot. Never let them get too dry because that weakens the plants and makes them more susceptible to black spot. *—Jennifer Mitten Algona, Washington*

**Roses need** fertilizer only during their growing season. In late summer or early fall, let them go dormant to prepare for winter. *—Mary Wilson, Wichita, Kansas*

**New rosebushes** should not be fertilized until after their first blooming period. *—John Frost Medina, Washington*

**Roses are easy** to grow, but many require a lot of care. If you're interested in growing them, contact the American Rose Society, P.O. Box 30,000, Shreveport LA 71130-0030 (telephone 1-318/938-5402) and ask for the local rose society closest to you. There are chapters throughout the country and even in foreign countries.

*—Bernie Roudybush Forsyth, Missouri*

**Hang a hummingbird** feeder above your rose-bushes to keep aphids away. I tried this and was delighted with the results. The birds cleaned the bushes of every single aphid before they moved on to the nectar in the feeder!
—*Joanne Craft-Lane*
*Sumter, South Carolina*

**For the best blooms**, plant roses in an area that gets at least 6 hours of full sun a day. —*Bill Ott*
*White Lake, Michigan*

**I mix ornamental** hot peppers in with all of my plants, including my rosebushes. The plants have seldom suffered from black spot. Since I don't use a fungicide, I'm convinced that the hot peppers keep black spot at bay. —*Jim Richings*
*Maydelle, Texas*

**Here are a few** tips to keep your roses beautiful throughout the growing season.

- In early spring, trim back the dead canes. Then fertilize the plants with granular rose food, working it lightly into the soil.
- Each month throughout the summer, fertilize using a balanced rose food.
- Make sure roses are well watered. To protect them from disease, water only at the base of the plant.

- To keep roses blooming throughout the growing season, trim off spent blooms.
- In more northerly areas, prune back to allow for winter protection. But main pruning should be done in spring.
- The winters in your area will determine how you should mound or cover your roses to protect them until spring. —*Jeanette Dalton*
*Mountain Grove, Missouri*

**There are roses** out there even for people who don't have the time or energy for constant pruning and spraying. You can find out about many hardy selections in books about old garden roses. These plants flourish with little or no care.

If you don't want to prune, plant a shrub rose. Also, I've learned it's better to start with a healthy, more expensive plant that requires minimal care than to be enticed by cheap low-quality plants.
—*Susan Menzmer*
*Angwin, California*

**As the temperatures** hover around freezing in fall, I lay my climbing roses down and cover them with leaves. I wrap the tea and floribunda roses with burlap, then fill their enclosure with leaves to a depth of 3 feet. Shrub and species roses need no winter protection, even where I live.
—*Priscilla Osgood, Bangor, Maine*

**Plant parsley** around your rose-bushes to deter aphids.
—*Patricia Murray, Niles, Ohio*

**Here's a method** to make new roses from bushes already growing on their own hardy root stock in your yard.

Cut a healthy tip about 5 inches long. Trim off the bottom leaves. Make a small hole in an out-of-the-way area of your garden and fill it with sphagnum moss. Put the cutting in the hole, water it and put a clean clear glass jar over it. (Be careful…watch that your plant does not overheat.)

As long as it's not too hot, you should have a healthy plant in about 6 weeks. Then uncover it and treat it like any other growing plant.

This works especially well with miniature roses. It can be done all summer long. I've even done it in fall and left the jar over the plant throughout the winter.

—*Jean Porn, Chicago, Illinois*

**Buy only high-quality** rosebushes. You get what you pay for, and a good bush will last a lifetime. Here are additional tips that work for me. Never spray water on the bushes, don't let them go into nightfall with wet foliage and use cypress mulch in your rose beds.

—*Merle Scoggins*
*Fort Worth, Texas*

**To control aphids** on rosebushes, poke three holes as close to the roots as possible. The holes should be about 6 inches deep. Put two mothballs in each hole, cover and water. In about a week, all the aphids should be gone, and they'll stay away the rest of the season.

—*Lillian Hilburn, Orosi, California*

**Roses need good** fertile soil that drains well but doesn't dry out too quickly. I use equal parts potting soil, sand and compost or peat for the ideal mix.     —*Mary Wilson*
*Wichita, Kansas*

**It's best to spray** roses in early morning so the foliage has time to dry before night. Never spray during the heat of the day. Give special attention to the underside of foliage, where most insects live and spores germinate.     —*John Frost*
*Medina, Washington*

**After a rosebush** blooms and the flowers die, I cut the stem with the flower down to the next leaf with 5 leaflets. The plant continues to

bloom into late summer and sometimes early fall.     —*Jan Grage*
*Centerville, South Dakota*

My cut roses never lasted long, and sometimes the buds didn't even open. Then I discovered Schultz Instant Liquid Plant Food, which has an easy-to-measure dropper. With 1 to 3 drops in the vase, the roses last 10 to 12 days, and all the buds open beautifully.
—*Ellen Teson*
*Tacoma, Washington*

This spring, I placed orange and grapefruit peels at the base of my tall rosebush. I got more blooms than ever before—30 at one time and 15 more a month later.
—*Mona Wichman*
*Rumson, New Jersey*

To rid roses of aphids, simply direct the spray from your garden hose underneath the leaves. This gets them off your plants...and since they can't fly, they don't return.
—*Joanne Craft-Lane*
*Sumter, South Carolina*

Don't rob rosebushes of nourishment by cutting canes prematurely in fall. Instead, create a collar around the base of the plant.

First, remove the bottom from a brown paper grocery bag and cut the remaining part open to form a 36- by 16-inch rectangle. Fold it lengthwise and wrap it around the base of the bush, securing it with duct tape. Surround this with chicken wire and shovel dirt into the center. This pre-

vents formation of mildew at the base and preserves food in the canes. In spring, remove the wire and roll it up to use again; discard the collars.     —*Michelene Rocco*
*Lemont, Illinois*

Always water well before and after applying granular fertilizer. If dry fertilizer gets on the leaves, rinse it off immediately.     —*John Frost*
*Medina, Washington*

Trellises for roses, vines or espaliered plants can be costly. So I make my own from fir strips that are sold at lumberyards or building supply stores for less than $1 each. These 1- by 2-inch strips are 8 feet long and can be horizontally nailed or attached to a fence or wall. I put them on a fence about 18 inches apart, then stain them to match.     —*Paul Peterson*
*Redding, California*

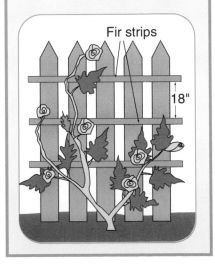

Fir strips

18"

## WORDS TO GROW BY

**After you've finished** working in the garden, wash your garden gloves while they are still on your hands. Hang the gloves to dry, and you'll have a clean pair for the next day of gardening.
—*Ann Proffit*
*Bellbrook, Ohio*

**Roses**, like people, need lots of water. Also, prune off all dead wood in early spring and repeat every other month.    —*Patricia Willingham*
*Dallas, Texas*

**In fall, we make** rose cages from chicken wire and fill them with grass clippings and chopped leaves. In spring, we remove all this and prune the bushes back to the green. We have beautiful blooms every year.  —*Kenny and Shirley Wackler*
*Covington, Ohio*

**In our thin** rocky alkaline soil, I feed my "rose mania" with *Rosa rugosas*. They're extremely hardy, insect- and disease-resistant and thrive in a wide range of climates and soils. They are suitable for hedges and shrubs. Except for deadwood, they don't need pruning, and many bloom repeatedly spring through fall.                   —*Geri Davis*
*Prescott, Arizona*

**Bare-root roses** should be soaked in water overnight before planting,
and the roots should not be exposed to drying sun or wind.
—*John Frost, Medina, Washington*

**Plant roses** at least 20 feet from the base of any large tree. Otherwise, the tree's roots may rob the roses of nutrients and moisture.
—*Bill Ott, White Lake, Michigan*

**The biggest mistake** many people make is choosing a rose only for its color or fragrance. A bit of education before you buy will make a big difference. A dead or diseased rose will *not* give you "that rosy feeling".          —*Mary Wilson*
*Wichita, Kansas*

**In areas** with mild winters, plant hardy types of rosebushes that can grow on their own roots. Then take cuttings when pruning the bushes back. I planted many cuttings in soil and soon had new plants. Also, I plant chives among my rosebushes to discourage aphids.
—*Julie Soileau*
*Marbury, Alabama*

**I live** in a warm area and am lucky enough to be able to garden in winter. Even so, aphids are still a challenge. I ward them off by planting garlic along my row of rosebushes in January, when I'm pruning. By spring, when aphids begin to attack, the garlic is nice and tall. They don't like the smell.

—*Dorothy Larson*
*Ontario, California*

**Before pruning roses** in spring, dig a 4-inch trench around them. Sprinkle in 1 or 2 tablespoons of granular ammonium nitrate fertilizer mixed with 1/3 cup of systemic rose food, then lay an overripe banana in the trench. Cover with dirt, mulch well and water *thoroughly*.
—*Helen Jones, Opelika, Alabama*

**In warmer areas**, this is a good way to prepare your roses for winter. I fertilize my roses with chicken litter in fall (once in spring, too) and also pile grass clippings around them. I never put anything else around my roses, and I've had many compliments on the big flowers and healthy bushes. —*Lorene Freeman*
*Star City, Arkansas*

**To enjoy** the beauty of roses without all the spraying and work that most roses take, plant easy-care varieties like Carefree Beauty, The Fairy and Carefree Wonder.
—*Laura Horning*
*Mifflintown, Pennsylvania*

**I feed my roses** with a slow release rose fertilizer (20-11-12) twice per growing season—in early spring and early summer. I like this formula because it has controlled-release nitrogen. —*Kathi Richards*
*Dundee, Ohio*

**Scratch 1/2 cup** of Epsom salts into the soil around each rosebush in spring. This encourages strong stems. Garlic planted among rosebushes is a great way to keep pests away. —*Linda Canfield*
*Saline, Michigan*

**Pruning** improves rosebushes. Unpruned roses bloom on small cane tips, go to seed and stop flowering. Even poor pruning is better than no pruning at all. The general rule is to prune strong-growing bushes moderately and weak ones severely.
—*John Frost*
*Medina, Washington*

**Rose roots** need ample room to grow, so dig a hole wider and deeper than the root systems. Make a cone of soil in the center of the hole and position the rose so its bud union—the knobby bulge at the top of the root system—is just below ground level. In colder northern states, you may need to plant the bud union deeper. —*Mary Wilson*
*Wichita, Kansas*

---

**Try planting** geraniums, especially white ones, in and around roses. This helps repel Japanese beetles. In the last 3 years, I've found less than a dozen beetles on my roses. —*Kathi Richards*
*Dundee, Ohio*

**To protect** rosebushes in cold climates like mine, cut them back to 6 to 8 inches in November. Then gently cover them with soft loose soil and add a layer of mulch hay at least 12 inches thick.

When the ground begins to thaw in spring, remove the mulch and soil from the crowns of the plants to allow new growth. Discard the old hay and tuck fresh hay loosely around and on top of the plants to protect them from surprise frosts.

After all danger of frost has passed, remove the hay and add well-composted horse or cow manure to the soil around the bushes. Be careful not to damage the roots.

—*Amy Wright Brill*
*Sutton, Vermont*

**My secret** to spectacular roses is feeding them. Every 2 years, I give each rosebush a cup of iron-based amendment. On the "between" years, I top dress the plants with composted turkey manure.

Every year, I give each bush a slow-release food pellet made for large trees. And twice during the growing season, I treat each plant with a cup of basic rose or flower food granules.

I don't water the plants with an overhead spray, so I haven't had problems with rust, black spot or fungal diseases. When aphids appear, I wait patiently and let the ladybugs take care of them.

—*Teresa Hansen*
*Elk Grove, California*

**For a stand-out** rosebush in late summer, plant a Paradise hybrid tea rose in your garden. It is known for its colorful foliage. Give it lots of water all summer long to keep it healthy.

To keep fungus from attacking this rose early in the season, use fungicides (follow label directions) and continue this treatment until fall.

—*Mary Bray*
*Comstock Park, Michigan*

**I like to mound** the soil in a ring around a rose plant so the water doesn't run off. Roses need plenty of water to grow those beautiful flowers. A good deep soaking once a week is usually enough.

—*Mary Wilson*
*Wichita, Kansas*

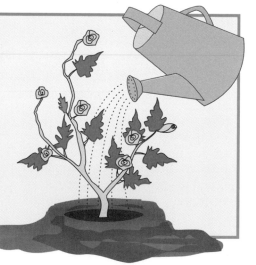

**To treat black spot** on roses, mix 1 tablespoon of baking soda, 2-1/2 tablespoons of horticultural oil and 1 gallon of water. Spray this solution on bushes when symptoms appear and every 1 to 2 weeks thereafter.
*—Laura Horning*
*Mifflintown, Pennsylvania*

**Because our winters** were cold, Dad always piled soil around the base of his roses to protect them. He didn't remove it until some green appeared on the stems above the soil line. *—Dorothy Kalinay*
*Van Horne, Iowa*

**Turn your rosebushes** into snowmen in the winter. Place recycled birdseed bags over the bushes and cover them with white plastic garbage bags. *—Yvonne Rhudy*
*Holland, Michigan*

**Don't throw away** the straw used to protect your roses during the winter months. Move it to a level area, such as your lawn, and run the mower over it to cut the stems into smaller pieces. Then incorporate the straw into your garden. It also makes excellent mulch.
*—Neil McGregor*
*Kamloops, British Columbia*

**To master** growing roses, it is important to pick the best location possible. I suggest planting rosebushes in a well-drained raised bed that gets at least 6 hours of sun daily.

Space hybrid tea roses 3 to 4 feet apart and mulch with straw, cypress or pine shavings. Prune in spring and water weekly throughout the summer.

To keep your roses beautiful, buy a systemic rose fertilizer and insect control combined. Use it once a month at the base of each plant and water well. Also, buy a fungicide to mix with water and spray your roses weekly (follow label directions).
*—Sheri Anderson Todd*
*Brundidge, Alabama*

**When planting roses**, locate a spot with sunlight, good drainage and no intruding tree roots. Good air circulation will minimize black spot and mildew problems. If existing drainage is bad, consider planting your rosebushes in a raised bed.
*—John Frost, Medina, Washington*

**Keep a shallow** trough around each rosebush in your garden. When it doesn't rain in summer, the bushes are easy to water, and they'll keep blooming until frost.
*—Mrs. B. Lukavik*
*Bangar, California*

**Here's how** to save a broken rose branch from a plant that grows on its own hardy root stock. Put a layer of rocks in the bottom of a plastic flowerpot. Fill the pot with soil and plant the broken branch. The rose will root in the pot, and you'll have a new rose to add to your garden or give away. *—Faye Henderson*
*Gaffney, South Carolina*

**Remove thorns** from cut roses by pushing sideways on them with your thumb. They'll pop right off. *—Mary Wilson Wichita, Kansas*

**A "system"** is the key to growing lovely roses. My system has rewarded me with several ribbons at local rose shows.

Prune rosebushes to 12 to 18 inches in spring. At this time, sprinkle granular food around the base of each bush. Continue to feed them once a month. (In cold areas, stop feeding by August 1.)

Once a week, cut off faded blooms and give your bushes a good drink of water. Then apply an all-purpose spray to combat insects, black spot and powdery mildew. That's it! *—Gerard Budzynski Shrewsbury, Pennsylvania*

**Phosphate fertilizer** (superphosphate or bone meal) is the only material that should be placed in a planting hole. Avoid high nitrogen or quick-release fertilizer. It will burn the roots and damage your rosebushes. *—John Frost Medina, Washington*

**Roses won't tolerate** "wet feet". Before planting a rose, pour 2 gallons of water into the hole to make sure it will drain away in a few minutes. *—Bill Ott White Lake, Michigan*

**I've found a way** to rid my roses of aphids without using chemicals. I planted garlic around the bushes and spray the roses twice a week with a concoction of 1 tablespoon of dishwashing soap, 1 tablespoon of cooking oil and 1 quart of water.

After I used this spray, the aphids disappeared and the leaves on the rosebushes now have a beautiful shine from the oil. *—Doris Frichtel Oceanside, California*

**Here are some tips** to consider when designing a rose garden:
- Locate the garden in the right area—roses grow best in full sun.
- Make sure you have enough space for each type of rose selected so the garden doesn't look overgrown in a few years.
- To add a personal touch, let each member of the family choose their own variety of rose.
- When designing the layout, think of additional roses and accents you'll want to add in the future.
- Combine miniature, bush, climbing and hybrid tea roses. They'll add interest to the garden.
- Don't forget to consider the amount of maintenance your garden will need. Choose a design and size that will fit your schedule. *—Bonnie Andersen Roundup, Montana*

# CHAPTER SIX

# UNBEATABLE COMBINATIONS

HERE are some odd couples that just may make your gardening a little easier. These combinations of plants seem to do better as teams than by themselves.

Some of these pairings keep critters and pests away, while others may help each other along as they grow. (Remember the hollyhock and morning glory idea mentioned on page 7?) Read on...we're sure you'll find the perfect combination to suit your own tastes and needs.

**Plant a few radish seeds** along with your beets, carrots and parsnips. The radishes will sprout first and mark the row until the other seeds come up.　　*—June Wescott Brewster, Nebraska*

**Some of my** favorite companion plants in the vegetable garden are: basil and tomatoes; horseradish and potatoes; dill and cabbage; cabbage and onions; chives and carrots; and summer savory and beans. These plants always do better when I plant them together.　*—Mildred Cordell Mechanicsburg, Ohio*

**With garden space** at a premium, I planted lettuce between my tomatoes. The tomato plants shaded the lettuce, which likes less sunlight and cooler temperatures. When it got too crowded, I just pulled all the lettuce for a final salad.
*—Theresa Walsh West Milford, New Jersey*

**Savory** planted in bean rows will keep bean beetles away, and mint (careful, it can be a weedy and aggressive plant) will deter ants, moths and black flies.　*—Sarah Baker Winchester, Virginia*

**Many people** grow carrots and radishes together. But I've found that when you pull a radish, you sometimes get a carrot, too. Now I grow my carrots with peas instead.

The shallow-rooted pea plants are easily pulled after the peas are picked, and the carrots keep growing.　　　*—Mary Schmidt Hawarden, Iowa*

**Sunflowers** planted across the middle of my garden provide shade and a windbreak for other plants. Just be careful not to plant pole beans or potatoes near them.
*—Kitty Rhodes Park Ridge, Illinois*

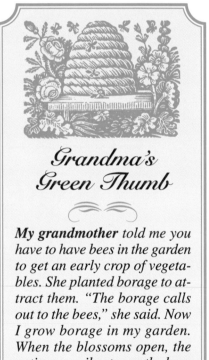

*Grandma's Green Thumb*

**My grandmother** told me you have to have bees in the garden to get an early crop of vegetables. She planted borage to attract them. "The borage calls out to the bees," she said. Now I grow borage in my garden. When the blossoms open, the entire row vibrates as the bees work the flowers. And I always have early vegetables—even with our short growing season.　　*—Nancy Stoddard Broadus, Montana*

**Plant mint** (careful, it can be a weedy and aggressive plant) between broccoli and cauliflower plants, and you'll never have those pesky green worms in the heads.
—*Mrs. Henry Foster*
*Waitsfield, Vermont*

**I plant irises** behind peonies. They flower at the same time and look pretty together. I also plant cosmos, tall marigolds and snow-on-the-mountain together. They look nice in bloom, and the marigolds help hold up the cosmos.
—*Celestus Lewis*
*Springfield, Kentucky*

**For a full day** of blooms, plant morning and evening plants together. For example, I plant four-o'-clocks in front of morning glories. That way, when the morning glories are past their glory, the multicolored four-o'clocks begin their fragrant and colorful show.
—*Marion King*
*Gloucester, Ontario*

**Plant zinnias** with morning glories. The vines will help hide the powdery mildew that often occurs on the zinnia leaves.
—*Lois Houskamp*
*Caledonia, Michigan*

**I always plant** spreading vines next to vegetables with short seasons. When the short-season vegetables are harvested, the vines can spread into those areas. Some good combinations include cucumbers with green beans, pumpkins with peas, squash with radishes and melons with spinach.
—*Deborah Moyer*
*Liberty, Pennsylvania*

**I save the seeds** from my poppies and sow them around my tulips when they start to come up. When the tulips are finished blooming, the poppies take over, and you don't notice the dying tulip foliage.
—*Lena Stratton*
*Superior, Wisconsin*

**Combine cucumbers** and morning glories on the same trellis. They do well together, and the yellow cucumber blooms and blue morning glories make a pretty combination.
—*Donna Scrudder*
*Broken Arrow, Oklahoma*

**I alternate rows** of carrots and onions. This keeps both carrot flies and onion maggots away.
—*Sue Gronholz*
*Columbus, Wisconsin*

**Nasturtiums and beans** are effective companion plants, enhancing and protecting each other's growth. And they complement each other on the table, too. Whenever I prepare fresh green, snap, wax, Roma or shell beans, I add a few decorative and delicious nasturtium blossoms to the serving bowl.
—*Chris Bernard*
*Lake City, Michigan*

**A great way** to hide dying tulip leaves is to plant the bulbs *behind* your perennials. After you enjoy the pretty tulip blooms, the perennials will hide their foliage. Hostas make especially good cover-ups.

*—Nancy Snyder*
*Willmar, Minnesota*

**We like to use** every inch of space in our garden. So where we plant a row of gladiolas, we plant seeds of low-growing plants, like violas, alyssum and moss roses. These plants shade the gladiola bulbs from the hot sun. And when they're finished blooming, we still have a pretty mix of colors starting again when the gladiolas bloom.

*—Jack and Luci Laughlin*
*Fort Wayne, Indiana*

**Here are two** combinations of plants that will add colorful interest in the vegetable garden.

When planting zucchini, make a hollow in the soil and plant three or four zucchini seeds in the center. Before covering them with soil, add a few nasturtium seeds on the outer rim of the hollow.

And when transplanting tomatoes, put marigold seeds at the base of each tomato plant you have staked. Together, they will create a pretty bed of golds, oranges and maroons. *—Clara Belle Tye*
*Washougal, Washington*

**Try planting parsley** with your carrots to deter carrot worms.

*—Sarah Baker*
*Winchester, Virginia*

**In spring**, I have a beautiful bed of white iris. Lantana comes up in the same bed after the iris has bloomed and lasts the rest of the summer. Besides being resistant to heat and drought, the lantana chokes out weeds. *—Clara Harden*
*Four Oaks, North Carolina*

**I experiment** with different combinations of garden flowers in a vase first. I'll plant the ones I like in my garden the following year.

*—Jerry Nelson*
*Raymond, Wisconsin*

**Plant nasturtiums** among vining plants, like pumpkins, cucumbers and squash, to ward off garden pests. It works with bottle gourds, too. Marigolds do the same when planted among cabbages and tomatoes.
*—Mary Mahn, Ravenna, Michigan*

**Borage or dill** will repel tomato hornworms. *—Sarah Baker*
*Winchester, Virginia*

**We alternate rows** of potatoes and bush beans in our vegetable garden. The beans repel Colorado potato beetles, and the potatoes repel Mexican bean beetles.

*—Edris Weinand*
*St. Cloud, Minnesota*

**I grow larkspur** in my rose garden to keep Japanese beetles away. It has delicate lacy foliage, and the heavenly blue flowers blend in beautifully with the roses. The larkspur reseeds itself from year to year.
—*Janet Morgan*
*Charlestown, Rhode Island*

**Mix carrot and radish** seeds together when planting. The radishes will mature first and harvesting them thins the carrots. It really works! My grandpa taught me this trick when I was a child, and I still use it to this day. —*Dorothy Stokes*
*Beloit, Wisconsin*

**My purple-flowering clematis** (the variety *Jackmanii*) is planted on an arbor alongside pink John Cabot climbing roses. I wind the stems together as they grow, and the plants will bloom beautifully together.
—*Becky Olson*
*Arden Hills, Minnesota*

**If you're interested** in companion planting, check out Louise Riotte's book *Carrots Love Tomatoes*, published by Garden Way. It's one of the best investments I ever made.
—*Patricia Willingham*
*Dallas, Texas*

**Planting a row** of petunias between green or yellow string beans seems to produce more beans—and it beautifies the garden, too. Plant the petunias at the same time you plant the bean seeds.
—*Marie and Jerry Braasch*
*Princeton, Illinois*

**I stopped planting** lettuce in rows years ago. Now I just tuck seedlings into any available space. It's amazing how much lettuce you can grow this way. Tuck it around vegetables that grow upright. They will provide shade. You can also plant it in rings around cabbage and cauliflower.

The lettuce is also good for the plants because it acts as a "living mulch", keeping the soil cool and moist. I plant different varieties throughout the season and have fresh salad nearly every day.
—*Weldon Burge*
*Newark, Delaware*

**Plant tomatoes** next to asparagus. The insects and worms that like asparagus don't like tomatoes, and those that feast on tomatoes can't stand asparagus.
—*Dee Hancock*
*Fremont, Nebraska*

**To repel bugs**, plant dill with green beans and radishes with melons, squash and cucumbers. Chives planted next to lettuce and peas will protect those vegetables from aphid damage. —*Malinda Mast*
*Charm, Ohio*

**Sage deters** both cabbage flies and carrot flies when planted between those vegetables.
*—Sarah Baker*
*Winchester, Virginia*

**To discourage** asparagus beetles, I plant parsley, calendula and bush basil around my asparagus bed. In addition to acting as an insect repellent, these plants make a pretty border and are edible, too.
*—Sue Gronholz*
*Columbus, Wisconsin*

**If you plan** to grow raspberries, select a fall-bearer and plant it next to elderberries. Ours produce fruit at the same time. The birds are too busy picking elderberries to bother the raspberries.
*—Gertrude MacMillan*
*Stockton, New Jersey*

**When planting** melon or pickle seed, put some radish seed in a small circle around each hill. When the radishes are ready to harvest, leave 2 or 3 in the ground. This keeps melon bugs away without dusting.
*—Dorothy Larsen, Audubon, Iowa*

**Protect fruit trees** from aphids and borers by planting chives around them.
*—Sarah Baker*
*Winchester, Virginia*

**I finally found** a combination of annuals that will survive northwest New Jersey's hot summer sun— African marigolds, red and pink verbena and vinca vines. They bloomed beautifully until the first fall frost.
*—Tina Jacobs, Wantage, New Jersey*

**I plant thyme** in different spots throughout my garden. It seems to enhance the aromatic qualities of other plants and herbs.
*—Kitty Rhodes*
*Park Ridge, Illinois*

**Plant a tomato** next to a sunflower that's about 2 feet tall. As the tomato plant grows, tie it to the sunflower stalk instead of a stake.
*—Robert Goodwin*
*Eastford, Connecticut*

**Grow garlic** between tomatoes, onions, beets, broccoli and roses. It will repel aphids, onion flies and mosquitoes.
*—Sarah Baker*
*Winchester, Virginia*

**I plant** dill in my tomato patch to keep bugs away. If you don't remove the dill seeds, they'll come up every year.
*—Evelyn Ough*
*Manchester, Connecticut*

**Plant marigolds** with your daffodils to create a long-lasting sunny border. Daffodils planted along our garden pathway make it look like the sun is shining even on cloudy days. When these blooms fade, the marigolds take over, adding color while hiding the browning daffodil foliage.
*—Dot Christiansen*
*Bettendorf, Iowa*

## Grandma's Green Thumb

*My grandma always planted a row of zinnias in her garden, with garlic here and there, to keep the bugs out.*
*—Rita Jemison*
*Ashland, Mississippi*

**To hide** browning leaves of morning glories, plant scarlet runner beans right next to them. That way, when the morning glory leaves begin to brown, the scarlet runners can share the color of their green leaves.
*—Rachel Maendel*
*Elka Park, New York*

**Plant climbing string beans** next to large sunflowers, such as Russian sunflowers. As the sunflowers grow, they create a trellis for the beans. And the sunflowers' seed heads make a nice treat for the birds that visit our yard in winter.
*—Mary Bertek*
*Traverse City, Michigan*

**To display** shade-loving impatiens with sun-loving plants, find old crates used at local orchards. Stand the crates on their sides to make display boxes out of them. Place potted impatiens in the crates (so they are shaded). Put potted petunias, geraniums, dahlias and zinnias on top for a pretty double-decker display of mixed plants.
*—Phyllis Reiss*
*Coopersburg, Pennsylvania*

**Try planting** *Crocosmia* "Lucifer" behind coreopsis "Moonbeam". It's stunning when the bright red crocosmia blooms cascade over the pale yellow coreopsis. And you don't have to plan the blooming time because Moonbeam is almost always in bloom.
*—Irene Jones, Chardon, Ohio*

**Morning glories** will climb hollyhocks' sturdy stems and give your garden double the color.
*—Vera Heimul*
*New Brighton, Minnesota*

**To keep birds** from attacking strawberries, I grow cacti in the same bed. This way the delicious fruits arc all mine. The birds don't even attempt to snack on them. To pick the berries, I use barbecue tongs. They work great.
*—Mary Hilgemann, Norwalk, Iowa*

**Tomatoes** love carrots. We set out one tomato, then a 4-foot row of carrots, then another tomato, etc., and put rows of carrots on either side. This produces larger tomato plants and bigger yields of both crops.
*—Lona Varner*
*Chino Valley, Arizona*

Try companion planting in the vegetable garden. The results are worth the effort.

I plant summer savory with beans. Sage works well with any member of the cabbage family. And you can't go wrong by planting basil with tomatoes. Not only do these plants grow better together, but the herbs I cook with the vegetables are right there when I harvest.

—*Margaret Harvey*
*Northumberland, Pennsylvania*

When a tree dies, you don't always have to cut it down. When I lost a crab apple, I planted morning glories around the base. The flowers used the tree for support—it was beautiful. —*Rachel Maendel*
*Elka Park, New York*

Try planting chamomile with your tomatoes. Since I started doing this, I've had more tomatoes and no bugs or worms. —*Kitty Rhodes*
*Park Ridge, Illinois*

I shade lettuce by planting it under a teepee of pole beans. The beans provide the shade needed by the tender lettuce plants.

—*Nancy Adams*
*Hancock, New Hampshire*

Plant nasturtiums with your potatoes to keep potato bugs away.
—*Sarah Baker*
*Winchester, Virginia*

I put several catnip plants in my potato patch to discourage flea beetles. But don't do this if white flies are a problem in your area…catnip can attract them. —*Sue Gronholz*
*Columbus, Wisconsin*

I plant chives in all of my raised strawberry beds. The chives keep it bug-free (but, unfortunately, not bird-free).
—*Gladys Waldrop*
*Calvert City, Kentucky*

Plant tomatoes near your asparagus to keep the asparagus bugs away. —*Minnie Nunemaker*
*St. Johns, Michigan*

Marigolds will deter insects if planted next to potatoes and tomatoes. Scented geraniums have the same effect when planted next to tomatoes.

—*Marie and Jerry Braasch*
*Princeton, Illinois*

Keep bugs from your rose plants by planting chives around them. It looks pretty, plus you can clip some of the chives for use in salads.
—*Nancy Morris, Greenwich, Ohio*

Keep Japanese beetles out of your grape arbor by planting rue, chamomile, tansy or catnip under it. —*Sarah Baker*
*Winchester, Virginia*

# CHAPTER SEVEN

# PICK OF THE CROP
# FRUITS AND VEGETABLES

BIGGER, BETTER AND TASTIER...who could ask for more from a vegetable garden or the fruit-producing plants in their backyard? Try a couple of these ideas and you may find yourself regularly sharing abundant crops with friends and relatives.

Fruits and veggies are a favorite subject of many of the gardeners who responded to our request for hints. And why not? What can be more fun than making a meal of the harvest grown in your own backyard?

**When my potted tomato plant** started to die, a neighbor told me to put a tea bag in the pot, cover it with a little dirt and add water.

To my amazement, the plant was green and growing again within a few days. It produced tomatoes like you wouldn't believe.

—*Mildred Britton*
*Glendale, California*

**Before the first frost**, pick any remaining green tomatoes and place them near ripe bananas or apples. They'll ripen almost right before your eyes. The results—and the taste—are amazing.

—*Dianne Hutton*
*Prince Frederick, Maryland*

**To keep gourds** from becoming moldy after harvest, don't pick them until frost has killed the vine. It's important to quickly remove the gourds because a hard frost will injure them.

—*B.C. Sterling*
*Addison, Alabama*

**To plant tomatoes** early in the season, I cut off the bottom of a 5-gallon plastic bucket with a saw and plant it about 6 inches deep in my garden. Then I'll place a tomato plant in the middle of the bucket.

This method has helped me grow fantastic tomatoes each year because I can put them in the garden early. The bucket protects the plants from the wind and frost. (When

**To conserve space**, plant seed potatoes 12 inches apart in alternate rows 10 inches apart, in a zig-zag design. (See diagram.)

Put about 30 inches between each set of two rows. That way you only have to till between the sets of rows. To cover the potatoes, rake half of the tilled area to one side and half to the other.

When I hill up my potato rows with the soil, I make the sides higher than the center. This helps trap water, allowing it to soak through the soil to the seed potatoes, rather than running off the hill.

—*Eugene Sommers, Hartville, Ohio*

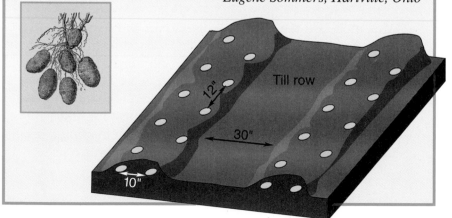

Till row

12"

30"

10"

there's the threat of frost, just cover the bucket with its lid.) It also makes it easy to water the plant. Just give them a good soaking inside the bucket.

I'll surround the buckets with wire cages to keep the plants controlled as they grow.

*—Bernice Miller*
*Akaska, South Dakota*

**At the very first sign** of brown rot, spray your grapes with a solution of 1 tablespoon baking soda and a gallon of water. I've never needed to use this spray more than once a season.

*—Eli Troyer*
*Apple Creek, Ohio*

**I don't have much room** in my vegetable garden, but I love cucumbers. This year, I put up a wood trellis with heavy twine running across it and planted cucumbers underneath. It worked great—the plants clung to the twine, and I had lots of cucumbers in a small space.

*—Virginia Smolich*
*Crest Hill, Illinois*

**We dig holes** for our tomatoes with a posthole digger, then plant them in 3-pound coffee cans. The can prevents cutworms, and the deep hole offers protection from the wind.

We feed with Miracle-Gro fertilizer once a week until the plants are about 18 inches tall. Then we surround them with wheat straw and build cages from concrete-reinforcement wire.

Last summer, my biggest tomato weighed in at 1 lb., 14.4 ounces. Our friends call me "The Tomato King".

*—Weldon Cox*
*Lawton, Oklahoma*

**To give green bean**, corn and pea seeds a head start, I presoak them in water overnight before planting. Then I plant green beans and corn together. As the beans grow, they use the cornstalks as supports.

*—Kathleen Couture*
*Waurika, Oklahoma*

**In mid-February**, I begin saving banana peels in a bag in the freezer. When it's time to plant tomatoes, I dig a ditch 2 inches deeper than required, lay the peels end to end and cover with dirt. Then I plant the tomatoes as usual. My tomato vines reached 8 to 10 feet, and the fruits were very sweet.

*—Kathy Mauller*
*Manchester, Missouri*

**Every year**, I plant four cherry tomato plants and harvest 1,000 to 1,400 tomatoes. My trick is preparation of the soil. In early November, I mix 5 pounds of cow manure and 40 pounds of topsoil into my 3-foot-by-8-foot patch. Letting the soil sit over the winter prevents it from burning the spring crop.

*—Greg Herd*
*Kingston, New York*

**Pour boiling water** on carrot seeds after planting and then cover with soil. Every seed will sprout and grow. Don't try this with other seeds; it won't work. —*Mildred Schlenz Vancouver, Washington*

**I always put lime in** the area of the garden where I plant tomatoes. This helps prevent blight and blossom-end rot. (This works in acid soils, so test your soil first before adding lime.) —*George Le Gore York, Pennsylvania*

**Epsom salts** can be used to provide magnesium sulfate to tomatoes, which increases yield and size. Mix 2 tablespoons Epsom salts in 1 gallon of water and apply 1 pint to each plant when blooming begins.
—*Sandy Traster Lambertville, Michigan*

**I've had fantastic results** with tomatoes by cutting the bottoms out of black plastic nursery pots and putting them around the plants. I also let 5-gallon buckets of water heat in the sun, then pour the warm water on the plants. —*Mrs. Bob Wilcox Wheatland, Wyoming*

**Sink a tin can** with both ends cut out next to your tomato plants (we use large chicken broth cans). Angle it toward the plants' roots. When you water and fertilize, pour into the can. This will take it directly to the plants' roots, prevent excess runoff and reduce your water bills.
—*Gene and Linda Smania Mendota, Illinois*

**Giant vegetables** were my father's trademark. At planting time, he surrounded each plant with a trough of granular plant food and gave each a good long soaking with the hose. He weeded once a week, watered plants when the soil was dry—and that was all. His tomatoes and bell peppers were the size of grapefruits every year!
—*Joanne Craft-Lane Sumter, South Carolina*

**Before digging carrots**, run the lawnmower over the row with the blade at the highest setting. This takes care of the tops and saves you a little time. —*Sue Gronholz Columbus, Wisconsin*

**Because our soil** is heavy clay, I had to come up with a new way to grow sweet potatoes.

So I use 5-gallon buckets to create raised gardens. I cut the bottoms off the buckets, set them on the ground and fill them with good quality soil. Then I plant sweet potatoes in the buckets after the last frost. I'll fertilize them about every 2 weeks.

In fall, just turn over the buckets to harvest your potatoes.
—*Joel McCormick Gainesville, Florida*

**Many fungus problems** are caused or spread by overhead watering. For garden rows, invest in soaker hoses. For individual plants, like tomatoes and peppers, bury a

**To prevent** cabbage butterflies from laying eggs on your cabbage leaves, cut a tomato cage 18 inches from the top and sink it 4 inches down around your cabbage plant. Then surround it with nylon netting, covering the bottom of the net with soil so it stays put.
—*Gladys Smith, Greenleaf, Idaho*

10- or 12-inch terra cotta pot next to each and plug the drainage hole with a rag. Cover the pots with screens to keep critters from falling in. To water, just fill the pot. The water seeps into the ground slowly and the foliage stays dry. A bonus—weeds really struggle from the lack of water between rows and plants.
—*Cheryl Smith*
*Rhinelander, Wisconsin*

**Prevent leaf spot** on your tomatoes by avoiding overhead irrigation. If this is the only way you can water, do it early in the day so the plants' leaves dry by evening.
—*Kathryn Vigliaturo*
*Esko, Minnesota*

**To boost production** of green pepper plants, I sprinkle them with an Epsom salt solution soon after planting. Mix 3 to 4 tablespoons in a gallon of water. Continue sprinkling until the peppers set.
—*Marilyn Brusven*
*Montevideo, Minnesota*

**I cover my cucumber bed** with landscaping cloth, cut out holes for planting and then cover the seeds with grass clippings (not from lawns with invasive grasses or recently treated with weed killers). This keeps weeds out, moisture in and the cucumbers clean.
—*Cathy Kostreba*
*Holdingford, Minnesota*

**Place a 6-foot post** between every third or fourth tomato plant. When the plants are about a foot tall, use baler twine to create a basket-weave pattern from post to post. When the plants are taller than the first row of twine, add another row. (Four rows will be enough for most tomatoes.) I find this works much better than tomato cages.
—*Virgil Downs*
*Mansfield, Ohio*

**Early blight** can cause tomatoes' lower leaves to develop spots, turn brown and drop, leaving fruit with no protection from sunscald. It's caused by fungus spores in the soil splashing onto the leaves. Keep this disease to a minimum by mulching, watering only at the plants' bases and pruning out the leaves 5 to 6 inches from the ground.
—*Sharon Foutch, Letts, Iowa*

**When you plant tomatoes**, add 1 tablespoon of Epsom salts to the hole. You not only get more tomatoes, but they taste sweeter, too.
*—Belinda Sipple*
*Burlington, Kentucky*

**After watching** my cucumber vines wilt and die for several years, I put wire fencing among the cukes and trained the vines to grow on it. The vines didn't wilt, and I had a good crop. It was easier to find the cucumbers, too. *—Rose Berg*
*Bangor, Wisconsin*

**Wrap your leftover** green tomatoes in newspaper and put them in a cool spot. When you want to use them, bring them out of storage, unwrap them and let them ripen in your kitchen. *—Jim Bailey Jr.*
*Long Beach, California*

**Make individual hothouses** for cabbage sets by cutting the bottom off 1-gallon black nursery pots. Place one pot over each set. Press the cut end into the ground 1 to 1-1/2 inches and remove when the temperatures begin to warm. My white cabbages were at least 7 pounds each, and the red cabbages were 5 pounds or more.
*—Daryl Olson, Nehalem, Oregon*

**My tomatoes grow** *around* a cage rather than inside it. Using heavy woven wire, I make a cage 5 feet tall and about 3 feet across. After staking it, I plant four tomatoes around it. As the plants grow, I tie them to the cage to keep the fruit off the ground and help them ripen sooner. I throw any grass clippings or leaves in the center of the cage to make compost and put the hose there for uniform watering. At the end of the season, the compost can be raked into the surrounding soil to improve it for next year's crop.
*—Albert Hensley*
*Vancouver, Washington*

**When planting root crops** like radishes, turnips and onions, sprinkle Epsom salts over the area to be planted, and you won't be bothered with bugs. *—Wallace Shelby*
*Lakemore, Ohio*

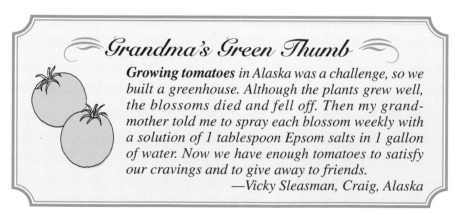

## Grandma's Green Thumb

*Growing tomatoes in Alaska was a challenge, so we built a greenhouse. Although the plants grew well, the blossoms died and fell off. Then my grandmother told me to spray each blossom weekly with a solution of 1 tablespoon Epsom salts in 1 gallon of water. Now we have enough tomatoes to satisfy our cravings and to give away to friends.*
*—Vicky Sleasman, Craig, Alaska*

70

**To freeze corn** without blanching, husk ears and brush off silk. Cut corn off cob. Melt 2/3 stick of margarine in electric skillet. Cook corn over high heat, stirring occasionally, for about 15 minutes. Cool by transferring corn to a pan with a fan directed on it. When cool, place in freezer cartons. This method prevents freezer burn. Once you've tried it, you won't do it any other way!
—*Virgil Downs*
*Mansfield, Ohio*

**You can treat** tomato transplants to a little light reading! Dig a hole just a bit bigger than needed and line with newspaper. It will absorb and hold more water for the plant's roots and will add nutrients as it decomposes. —*Mildred Sherrer*
*Bay City, Texas*

**Place unripe melons** on small tin cans turned upside-down—empty tuna cans work great. This keeps them off the cool ground, and the metal soaks up the sun's heat. I believe it helps the melons ripen faster and taste sweeter. —*Sue Gronholz*
*Columbus, Wisconsin*

**If you have** cold winters, cover strawberry plants in September with a season extending fabric (sold under the names Reemay and Frost Blanket). Then remove it in April. Research has shown this practice can increase yields as much as 75%.
—*Joyce Cooksey*
*Braintree, Massachusetts*

**Start leeks and onions** inside in January or February. When they're about 4 inches tall, cut them back to about 2 inches.

I continue to repeat this practice until they're ready to set out in April. This method makes the seedlings sturdier.
—*Ellen and Roger Caywood*
*Olympia, Washington*

**Before a freeze**, we pick all the partially ripe and even green tomatoes and put them in a single layer in a brown paper grocery bag. We close the bag with a clothespin and bring it indoors. In just a few days, the tomatoes are ripe.
—*Mrs. Calvin Hopper*
*Isle, Minnesota*

**For easier pea-shelling**, blanch the pods for 1 or 2 minutes or until you hear several pop. Immerse immediately in cold water, then strip the pods. The peas fall right out. Then drop the shelled peas in blanching water for 1 to 2 more minutes. Now they're ready for the freezer.
—*Almeda Campbell*
*Bolckow, Missouri*

**When harvesting** broccoli heads, cut the stalks at an angle to prevent the remaining stalk from filling with water and decomposing. The side shoots can then produce better broccoli. —*Deborah Moyer*
*Liberty, Pennsylvania*

**Eliminate bugs** and help with community recycling efforts by planting squash, cucumbers or melons in discarded tires.

Dig a hole, fill it with soil and add compost or manure. Set the tire on top and fill the tire with soil.

I started this to provide raised beds for heat-loving plants. But I discovered another benefit—I never had another squash or cucumber beetle. Believe me, I used to have plenty! —*Katherine Stanwood*
*Ashby, Massachusetts*

**Tie onions** in old pantyhose, using a clothespin or twist-tie to keep them from touching each other. Then hang them in a cool dry basement. I've kept Vidalia onions for 10 months this way. —*Dale Bahr*
*Manistee, Michigan*

**When planting vegetables**, I make a 2- to 3-inch ridge on both sides of the row. When I water the plants on dry summer days, the ridge works as a natural dike to keep the water where I want it.
—*Susie Fisher*
*Lewistown, Pennsylvania*

**Before planting** peppers, cucumbers and summer squash, cover the soil with black plastic. Cut holes in it to plant the vegetables. The plastic keeps the  weeds down and generates heat, which produces earlier healthier plants. —*June Hadland*
*Chehalis, Washington*

**When planting carrots** or lettuce, mix the seeds with dry used coffee grounds before planting. It makes planting the tiny seeds to these vegetables much easier.
—*Kathleen Couture*
*Waurika, Oklahoma*

**Carrot seed** is very fine, often dries out and takes 10 days to 2 weeks to sprout. I cover newly planted rows in my garden with strips of wood lath to keep the area moist and prevent the seeds from blowing away. In just over a week, I usually have sprouts and remove the lath. By sowing sparsely, there is no need to thin the rows, either.
—*Thomas Gay*
*Three Lakes, Wisconsin*

**We drive stakes** every 8 feet in our double row of peas and tie strong cords between them. The first cord is about 4 inches off the ground; we add more cords as the peas grow. This keeps the wind from whipping the vines. It helps at picking time, too. —*Thelma Carpenter*
*Great Bend, Kansas*

**I don't plant** green beans until I've harvested all my peas. I pull up the pea vines, till that row, then plant the beans, generally around July 1. I harvest three times more beans this way because the peas add nitrogen to the soil. The beans aren't disturbed by bothersome bean beetles either. That's because they're planted when the insects are past their prime.

—*Virgil Downs*
*Mansfield, Ohio*

**Want to raise** *big* tomatoes? Build a "tomato arbor"!

I did by rolling up 5-foot-wide sheets of concrete-reinforcement mesh (with 6 x 6 inch squares) to make eight cages.

Then I planted tomatoes in two rows, with 4 feet between rows. I removed all but the top two or three leaves from 12-inch tomatoes and planted them 11 inches deep with multiple time-delay fertilizer and mulch in the bottom of the hole.

Then I covered each plant with a cage and anchored each cage to the ground with No. 9 wire.

I placed wire mesh across the two rows and attached it to the tops of the cages with wire for stability.

With the tomatoes in the cages, I didn't need to tie them. I removed all the suckers until the plants were 2 feet tall. When the plants were 7 feet tall, I laid them over onto the mesh for a grape-arbor effect. The tomatoes continued growing, and I could pick them from overhead.

—*James Reinhardt, Alton, Illinois*

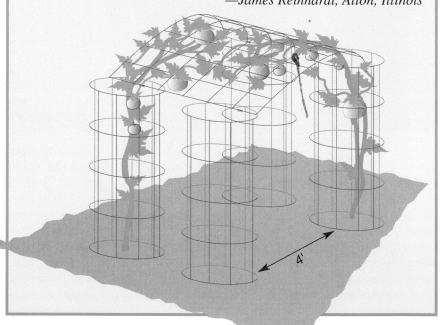

**Leave parsnips** in the ground until after the first hard frost. They'll be much sweeter.
—*Patricia Murray, Niles, Ohio*

**Here are my tips** for growing great tomatoes. Since they are heavy feeders, provide them with plenty of compost. Water them at ground level, never from the top. And always water deeply. —*Marjorie Carey Freeport, Florida*

## Grandma's Green Thumb

*Grandmother Julia always advised me to wrap strips of newspaper around the roots of cabbages before planting. This prevents cutworms from getting at the plant.*
—*Lori Woitalla Hillman, Minnesota*

**By trial and error**, I've found several varieties of vegetables that grow well in central Florida, an area where the soil is very sandy.

Bodacious Hybrid, a supersweet corn, outperforms all others I've tried and is resistant to earworms.

Fanfare Hybrid cucumber produces abundantly when picked often. Derby Bush snap beans produce a large harvest over an extended period. For a mildew-resistant summer squash, try Butterstick Hybrid.
—*Chris Stephan, Sebring, Florida*

**In northern areas**, place thick layers of newspaper between rows of garden vegetables and wet down. Then, when you cut the grass, bag the clippings and spread over the papers. You'll have a weed-free garden, and after spring tilling, it will be amazingly rich and dark.
—*Alfred Mullett, Millersburg, Ohio*

**Purple-podded bush beans** are cold-tolerant, productive and a breeze to harvest. The beans turn green when cooked, so I throw a few of them into the pot when I'm blanching regular green beans for freezing. When the color changes, I know the beans are blanched.
—*Weldon Burge, Newark, Delaware*

**I save** gallon-size milk jugs and punch a couple of holes in the bottom of each one. About once a month, I put a tablespoon of Miracle-Gro fertilizer in each jug, fill them with water and set them near my tomatoes, melons, etc. It gives them a good boost.
—*Miriam Christophel Battle Creek, Michigan*

**My mom** grew potatoes by planting just the thick peels that had eyes.
—*Dorothy Kalinay Van Horne, Iowa*

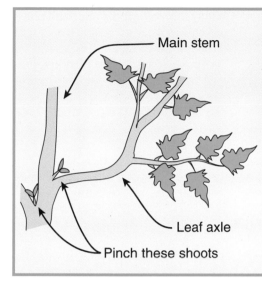

Main stem

Leaf axle

Pinch these shoots

**For earlier fruit** on your tomato plants, check regularly for little shoots that appear between the stem and leaf axle. Remove these by pinching between the finger and the thumb when they're about 3/4 inches long.

Also pinch off the top of the plant at the end of summer. Now it can ripen fruit instead of growing taller. *—Mrs. Jake Milles Shipshewana, Indiana*

**For a nice mixture** of cucumbers throughout the growing season, we grow several varieties including early- and late-maturing, as well as pickling and slicing types. We also plant at least two varieties of potatoes so there's less chance of crop failure. We usually end up with 500 pounds of potatoes for two families' winter use. For a good crop, be sure to use certified seed potatoes.

*—Ellen Gaugler Hoselaw, Alberta*

**It's easy** to get 5 or 6 heads of cabbage from one plant. Just cut off the first head when mature. Be sure to leave lower leaves attached to the roots. Within a few weeks, you'll notice multiple heads have started to form.

*—Kim Bednarowski Pickett, Wisconsin*

**When sweet corn** starts to silk, put a drop of mineral oil right in the center of the silk. This will keep worms out of the corn.

*—Mary Tempel and Irene Reyelts Wilmot, South Dakota*

**Before planting** beet seeds, spread them on waxed paper and roll them with a rolling pin. This crushes the outside husks, helping the seeds germinate sooner.

*—Irene Girard Claremont, New Hampshire*

**To water a plant** without wetting the leaves, sink cans with holes punched in the bottom on two sides of the plant. Then fill the cans with water. The moisture goes directly to the roots. This works especially well with tomatoes, which can develop a fungus from overhead watering. *—Mrs. David Sharkey Creswell, Oregon*

**Epsom salts** and borax can sweeten cantaloupes. Mix 7 tablespoons Epsom salts and 4 tablespoons borax in 5 gallons of water. Spray when the plants begin to vine and again when cantaloupes are baseball-sized. —*David Van Ness Salem, Ohio*

**Our family** loves brussels sprouts. But at harvest time, the brussels sprouts closest to the ground were too big, and those near the top were too small. Now I completely remove the top third of the plant in early September. This directs energy into the sprouts, which become larger and more uniformly sized.
—*Deborah Meyer Liberty, Pennsylvania*

**In late March,** cut the ends off a few sweet potatoes, put each in a can of water and set in a warm sunny spot. When there's lots of green

**In spring**, I plant sweet corn every 2 weeks. Then I have fresh ears right up until freezing weather arrives.
—*Henry Chachulski Dorr, Michigan*

foliage, break off the slips and place several in a jar of water. Roots will grow on their own.

Several days before planting, prepare a long hill 1 foot high. Plant slips 12 to 18 inches apart and keep the hill moist and weed-free.
—*Frances Hill, Lebanon, Kansas*

**To keep** white butterflies off my cabbage, I cover them with Reemay or other season-extending fabrics.
—*Sharon Colden Warroad, Minnesota*

**I plant beans** in spring, then again in July. That way we have some to harvest in October. —*Nita Price Lisbon, Iowa*

**I let cucumber plants** climb a trellis made from chicken wire and plastic drainpipe. It keeps the cucumbers cleaner, straighter and away from hungry gophers.
—*Holly Keller Luxemburg, Wisconsin*

**When tomatoes** begin to bloom, I lightly brush the center of the flowers with a watercolor paintbrush to distribute the pollen. In a few days, tiny tomatoes develop. This also works on eggplants, cucumbers and other similar plants.
—*Mabel Lade, Kearney, Nebraska*

**I like to put** a thick layer of newspapers under each watermelon and muskmelon to lift them off the ground a bit. This seems to keep insects from damaging them.
—*Neva Mathes, Pella, Iowa*

**For the easiest** potato harvest, just drop potato eyes on tilled soil and cover with at least 6 inches of rotted hay.

When you want new potatoes, just lift the hay, pick up what you need and carefully replace the hay.

To harvest mature potatoes, rake the hay aside. The potatoes are much cleaner, and you don't damage any with a potato fork. —*Linda Cotten Columbia,Tennessee*

**To grow garlic** in a warm area, I plant a large clove 2 inches deep in autumn. As soon as the plant sends up a bloom, I cut it off. This helps produce larger cloves.

When leaves turn yellow in spring, the garlic is ready to harvest. I know this method works because my elephant garlic won first place at the state fair. —*Lou Crowder Bethany, Oklahoma*

**Just before** cucumber vines start to run, put a wire cage over each stalk. The vines will run on the cage, and the cucumbers won't rot from being on the ground. They're easier to pick, too. —*Lynwood Hyler Batesburg, South Carolina*

**I grow my cucumbers** on a "U" shaped trellis made from wire fencing (the curve is on top). This makes for easier picking, cleaner pickles and a lot less kneeling.
—*Kim Kramer Oshkosh, Wisconsin*

**I sprinkle** lettuce and radish seeds on the ground (even on top of snow) in fall, after the first hard freeze. They come up first thing in spring.
—*Lora Gerlach Parkston, South Dakota*

**When my tomato vines** have lots of blossoms but the fruits are slow in coming on, I pollinate them with a Q-Tip. Just twirl gently in the center of each blossom. Tomatoes will appear in a few days.
—*Robert Jorclet Missouri Valley, Iowa*

**When freezing weather** threatened our second crop of plum tomatoes—they were all green—we tossed them in a brown paper bag with a couple of green apples. In 2 to 3 weeks, we had ripe red tomatoes, and they had wonderful flavor. —*Gail Grimson Big Bear City, California*

**One day a friend** helping us in the garden sprinkled some loose dirt over our cabbage plants. When we asked why, he explained it kills worms without having to use chemicals. It works! We've used his trick every year since.
—*Drusilla Van Damme Atkinson, Illinois*

I grow lots of leeks for the farmer's market. Rather than blanch the stalks with soil, I use marsh hay. This keeps them much cleaner and saves a lot of time washing them after harvest. —*Sue Gronholz*
*Columbus, Wisconsin*

Give pea seeds a head start by soaking them in water overnight before planting. This works with bean and corn seeds, too. —*Elsie Burris*
*Prineville, Oregon*

To protect tomato plants from wind, splashing rain and wilt, cut 4- to 5-inch holes in the bottoms of plastic grocery sacks and slip them inside the tomato cages.
—*Bobbie Jones*
*Huntington, Texas*

I save eggshells all year, then crush them in spring and mix them into the soil around my tomatoes. Planting sweet basil with or near the plants also seems to improve the yield. —*Julius Frank*
*Wolsey, South Dakota*

My husband has several tips for growing beautiful cantaloupes. Give them plenty of room, watch their color, be careful where you walk and don't pick until the stem attached to the vine begins to dry out.
—*Phyllis Jewsbury*
*Millstadt, Illinois*

For large tomatoes, use a good fertilizer, such as 12-12-12. Remember, the larger the plant grows, the more food and water it will consume. —*Lee Ball*
*North Canton, Ohio*

Planting a marigold between tomato plants helps keep aphids and other insects away. I rarely have needed to use insecticide.
—*James Burton*
*Mount Juliet, Tennessee*

In spring, when setting out garden plants, sow some seeds for the same vegetables. Your garden will last much longer, and you'll have plenty of good food in the fall.
—*Rita Hoffman, Burgoon, Ohio*

I have no place to store carrots at the end of the garden season, so I cover them with 1-1/2 to 2 feet of leaves. The ground underneath doesn't freeze, so I can harvest as needed. —*Robert Koster*
*Gretna, Nebraska*

If your tomatoes have a lot of vine but little or no fruit, you're fertilizing them too much.
—*Lee Farrell*
*Bakersfield, California*

When watermelons were ready to pick on our South Dakota farm, Dad always shoved one deep into a haystack so it wouldn't freeze. Months later, he'd bring it out for a Christmas treat. It tasted like it was fresh from the vine. —*Knute Storlie*
*Sun City, California*

**When transplanting tomatoes**, start with healthy dark-green plants with sturdy stems 10 to 12 inches high. Dig a hole deep enough to bury the entire stem. Mix 3 tablespoons Epsom salts into soil at the bottom. Set in plant—removing lower leaves and gently loosening any matted roots—and fill halfway with soil, pressing it around roots.

Fill hole with water to settle loose soil around roots. When water is absorbed, fill with soil several inches from top and soak again. Fill indentation with water as needed until you see new growth on top. Roots will grow out all along the buried stem.                   *—Jesse Sholes*
*Williamsport, Pennsylvania*

**We mulch** our raspberry patch with "wool tags"—the wool that's discarded when sheep are sheared. When it rains, the manure is washed out of the wool, so the plants get fertilized, too.    *—Bonnie Ashcroft*
*Lions Head, Ontario*

**Our potato harvest** always includes some very small ones I don't want to peel and scrub. So I wash off as much soil as possible, then put them in the washing machine for about 5 minutes. Then I cook them until they're crisp-tender, shred in a food processor and freeze for hash browns.    *—Marlene Smalldridge*
*Princeton, Idaho*

**I dehydrate everything**—tomatoes, peppers, squash, herbs, onions, etc.—and store them in the freezer. We make cream cheese spread with

**We enjoy fresh carrots** all winter. Here's how. Cut the bottom off a 5-gallon pail and bury it in the ground. Dry carrots well and pack the best ones tightly into the pail, with the pointed ends down. Don't pack any with blemishes or nicks from the shovel. When the pail is full, put the lid on and top with a brick. You'll have good crisp carrots through March and April.
*—Ada Marie Miller*
*Millersburg, Ohio*

dried tomatoes, basil, peppers and garlic. I also make soup mix with vegetables, herbs and bouillon. Dehydrated squash "chips" are great for dipping.    *—Cindy Bush*
*Roseville, California*

**We put** 2-liter soft drink bottles of water upside-down in the soil next to our melon and squash plants to help them through hot dry weather.
*—Becky Elliott*
*White Cloud, Michigan*

**At harvest time**, I cut cabbage close to its base to double my crop (cut above the lower leaves). Smaller heads, called cabbage buds, will form where the first one was removed.    *—Kathleen Couture*
*Waurika, Oklahoma*

79

**I plant potatoes** 3 or 4 inches deep, then mulch the entire patch with 8 to 12 inches of grass clippings (not from lawns with invasive grasses or recently treated with weed killers). I have no potato bugs, and the potatoes are easy to harvest.　　　*—Dee Hancock*
*Fremont, Nebraska*

**Pick** vegetables frequently. Some plants, including summer squash, cucumbers and peppers, will stop producing if you let them mature or go to seed. Swiss chard leaves will get large and tough if left too long.
*—Betty Brockbank*
*Ojai, California*

**To harvest onions,** wait until the tops are mostly dead. Dig out the onions, brush off loose dirt and spread them in a dry place. When well-dried, remove remaining dirt and plant tops. Store in mesh bags

**In late summer,** I start pinching off the tops of tomato plants and the ends of pumpkin vines. This seems to help fruit already on the plant get bigger and better.
*—Wanda Burrer*
*Wing, North Dakota*

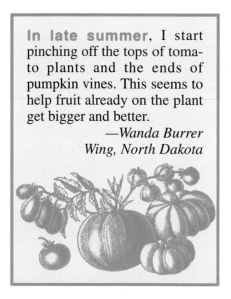

and hang in a cool dry place safe from freezing. Check frequently for spoilage.　　　*—Jerry Troyer*
*Glenford, Ohio*

**For sweeter melons,** reduce watering a week before picking. Water right after the first picking, then hold off again when the next batch is ready to harvest.
*—Betty Brockbank*
*Ojai, California*

**Want** a *square* pumpkin, squash or cucumber? Place the small vegetable in a half-gallon milk carton. As it grows, it will take on the shape of the carton.　　*—Neta Liebscher*
*El Reno, Oklahoma*

**Soak melon seeds** in strong tea. That gets them up and growing fast.
*—Ruth Twiss, Wray, Colorado*

**My dad** used this method to grow tomatoes and melons, and I also use it for gourds. Dissolve 10-10-10 fertilizer in water and soak corncobs for 4 to 5 days. Dig a hole 24 inches deep and 18 inches wide, then put a 6-inch layer of cobs in the bottom. Water the cobs, cover with soil, then put in plants and soak with water. The cobs hold moisture and enrich the soil as they decay. I use the same hole over and over for years.　　　*—Mamie Beam*
*Lexington, North Carolina*

**My husband** uses the lawnmower to cut down the canes of our fall-bearing red raspberries to a height of 4 inches. The new canes that come

*Grandma's Green Thumb*

**Over 50 years ago**, an "old-timer" gave my mother this hint for better carrot yields. After putting seeds in a row, do not cover with dirt. Instead, walk down the row. That presses the seed into the soil just enough. —*Carolyn McGuire Rumford, Maine*

up produce lovely berries from August until frost. —*Ethel Hagenbuch Utica, Illinois*

**To grow** abundant large potatoes and other vegetables, till horse manure sparingly into the soil in fall. Then add composted manure in spring. —*Edwin Kessler College Place, Washington*

**When my** green pepper plants begin to blossom, I put several drops of honey on each plant. This attracts the bees, which pollinate the plants. I repeat several times as the peppers blossom and get more and larger peppers than my neighbors. —*Ruth Griffin Randolph, New York*

**When our** cabbage plants start to form heads, I sift a little flour into the center of each plant. When the dew falls in the evening, bugs get stuck in the flour and harden. Goodbye cabbage worms and bugs! —*Edith Thomas, Portland, Oregon*

**To prepare soil** for a tomato seedling, dig a hole 18 inches in diameter and 12 inches deep. Save the dirt and pulverize it. Toss in a handful each of agricultural lime (if needed for acid soils), Epsom salts and vegetable fertilizer, then return the soil to the hole and plant the seedling. —*Robert Carver Athens, Georgia*

**"Tickle" your tomatoes** so seedlings don't get tall and spindly.

I transplant the seedlings to peat pots, set them in groups and give each plant 50 strokes with a postcard twice a day. This makes the stems thick and sturdy, and the plants don't grow as tall. —*Fred Aude Oak Creek, Wisconsin*

**After your peas** stop producing, cut them down with the lawnmower. Water several times and watch them start to produce again. —*George and Sarah Baker Winnsboro, Texas*

**Plant vegetables** in compost instead of putting them in black dirt. This gives them a better start and plenty of nutrients for a productive garden. —*Michael Hamilton Gilbertsville, Pennsylvania*

**Tristar strawberries** grow very well for us. They don't over-winter well to get a June harvest, but once they settle in, they give strawberries all season long. We had a crop in August, another in October and still had berries November 1.
—*Irene Jones, Chardon, Ohio*

**If frost threatens** and your hot peppers aren't ripe yet, pull out the whole plant and hang in a frost-free garage or shed. The peppers will continue ripening for several weeks. This works especially well for chilies and cayennes.
—*Sue Gronholz*
*Columbus, Wisconsin*

**For great tomatoes**, pinch off the plant's lower leaves before planting. Then dig a trench long enough to fit almost the entire length of the plant. Angle the plant downward so its roots are in the deepest section of the trench. Only the top leaves should be above ground level. This helps develop a strong root system. As the plant grows, pinch off suckers so the plant's energy is devoted to the fruit.     —*Theresa Walsh*
*West Milford, New Jersey*

**Plant a banana peel** with pepper plants. It makes the roots nice and strong.     —*James Grisdale*
*Mount Pleasant, Michigan*

**For a bigger** pepper crop, mix 1-1/2 to 2 teaspoons Epsom salts in a pint of water and spray on blossom-ing plants. Repeat 3 to 4 times at 7-day intervals.     —*David Van Ness*
*Salem, Ohio*

**Plant cucumbers** inside a wire cage. The vines grow up the cage and when they're ripe, just reach through the cage and pick nice clean cucumbers.     —*Betty Jean Rogers*
*Beason, Illinois*

**The trick** to growing tender celery is in the blanching process. It is really simple in northern areas like mine. Wrap each plant loosely at the end of July with black felt roofing paper cut 9-by-15 inches. Tie with twine. Then remove at harvest time.

It's cool enough here that the plants don't get heat damaged, but it doesn't hurt to keep a close eye on them.     —*George Hawk*
*Davison, Michigan*

**Mix seeds** from several different types of leaf lettuce in a plastic bag. Then plant one foot of a row each week. This will give you a continuous supply of "mixed greens" all summer.     —*Wendy Booth*
*Leechburg, Pennsylvania*

**My husband**, Derek, has a row of cinder blocks that holds a different herb plant in each hole. It makes an unusual border—and a productive one, too.     —*Carol Ann Deakin*
*Bethesda, Maryland*

**For faster development** of tomatoes and peppers, put 2 table-spoons of Epsom salts in one gallon of water. Apply to each plant as the blooms appear.

And for potato plants, remove the flowers so the plant's strength goes directly to the potato.

—*Joan Amato*
*Downsville, New York*

---

## WORDS TO GROW BY

**Here's an old rule** that still holds true: "Sow hardy vegetables when apple blossoms show pink; sow tender vegetables when lilac blossoms begin to show color."

—*Mrs. Calvin Hopper*
*Isle, Minnesota*

---

**Dip large tomatoes** into a kettle of boiling water for about a minute to help ease peeling. It works great. But don't try this with cherry tomatoes. All you'll get is mush.

—*Cathie Huguenin*
*Stevensville, Montana*

**To prevent tomatoes** from splitting, dig a hole about 6 inches from the plant, 4 to 6 inches deep. Pour in 1 tablespoon of Epsom salts, cover with dirt and thoroughly water. Since doing this, we no longer have tomatoes that split.

—*Brenda Trumps-Robinson*
*Sulphur, Louisiana*

**I plant butternut squash** and harvest them early to use like we would use zucchini. Then, when we've had our fill, we'll let the rest of the vine grow into the regular butternut squash and use these for pies and other favorite recipes.

—*Chris Miller*
*Montezuma, Georgia*

**To remove** worms from broccoli, swish the head of the plant in a sink full of hot water before cooking. Adding salt will help, too. The worms come right out.

—*Catherine Gall*
*Worland, Wyoming*

**To protect our tomatoes** and peppers from late-season frost, we used plastic garbage bags tied to the plants' cages. They saved our crop this past year.

—*Paul and Marilyn Spencer*
*Davenport, Iowa*

**In areas** with a long growing season, here's a tip for a longer tomato harvest. When you prune the side branches off your tomato plants, save them to plant in your garden. The cuttings will root easily. And when your first tomato plants are done producing, the cuttings will carry on where the first ones left off.

—*Marsha Melder*
*Shreveport, Louisiana*

**Here's how to enjoy** fresh tomatoes long after the first frost. Pick green tomatoes, wrap them in newspaper, put a layer or two in a box and store them in a cool dark place. Check occasionally for those that have ripened or spoiled.

—*Patricia Murray, Niles, Ohio*

**When washing lettuce**, place a small amount of vinegar in the water—about 1 tablespoon per gallon of water. The sand and dirt slip off the leaves better than they do in plain water.

*—Monica Hutson*
*Byron, Minnesota*

**I plant butternut** squash right in my compost pile. The results are excellent. *—Helen Costello*
*Chicopee, Massachusetts*

**Freeze whole tomatoes** on a cookie sheet in your freezer. Once they're frozen, store them in the freezer in zippered plastic bags. Take the tomatoes out as needed to add to soups or stews. Thaw them under hot water and the skin will just slide off. *—Susan Brown*
*Foristell, Missouri*

**When a volunteer** watermelon sprouted in our yard, the vine climbed our fence. A watermelon began growing part of the way up the fence. Afraid the heavy melon would break the vine, we put the melon inside the leg of a pair of pantyhose and tied it to the fence. It continued to grow and ripen.

*—Mrs. Harry Shotsman*
*Knox, Tennessee*

**Place cheesecloth** over cucumber and melon seedlings to foil beetles. The cloth can be secured to the ground using wire coat hangers. Just cut the hangers into 6-inch pieces, then bend them in half. (They'll look like large hairpins.) These pins can also be used to hold cloth over a newly seeded lawn.
*—Elizabeth Stephens, Dayton, Ohio*

**When my** tomato plants are still lush, I take cuttings from the ones that have produced the best tomatoes. I plant the cuttings in containers, then move them indoors and care for them at a sunny window or under a florescent (or grow) light throughout the winter. Don't forget to gradually harden them off to the outdoor climate before planting in spring. *—Patty Larson*
*Stacy, Minnesota*

**For really big** veggies, try my method. I dig planting holes 8 to 10 inches deep and fill with well rotted manure. In the middle, I make a second hole and fill with topsoil. I'll plant my seedlings in the topsoil. And when the weather warms, I'll mulch the garden to hold the moisture and keep the weeds down.
*—Bridena Fink*
*Centerville, Pennsylvania*

**To get** large watermelons on your vines, take a pair of scissors and snip the end of the vine after 3 or 4 flowers appear. This will give you a couple of full-sized watermelons rather than a bunch of small softball-sized ones.

Throughout the season, cut the vine off 3 or 4 inches past your flow-

ers. They grow so fast, this will become almost a daily routine.
—*Jim Bailey Jr.*
*Long Beach, California*

**In the hot** humid South, we're able to extend the life of our tomato plants by planting them deep. We start ours from seed and let them reach 12 to 15 inches before setting them out. Then we use a posthole digger to make a hole 2 feet deep. We add fertilizer and place the plant in the hole so two-thirds of it is covered with soil.     —*Florence Black*
*Seminary, Mississippi*

**After okra seeds** sprout, do not overwater the plants. They require less water than many other vegetables.     —*Helen Costello*
*Chicopee, Massachusetts*

**When we finish** planting potatoes, we scatter radish seed over the patch and rake it in. They're usually up and eaten by the time the potatoes pop through the ground. The radishes grow faster this way than when I planted them in rows because they have room to expand.
—*Drusilla Van Damme*
*Atkinson, Illinois*

**We don't need a root cellar** to preserve our bountiful carrot crop. My husband buries a galvanized tub up to its rim in soil, then fills it with carrots. The tub is covered with a sheet of plastic and then topped with hay. We enjoy fresh carrots right up until springtime.
—*Katherine Malboeuf*
*Moosup, Connecticut*

**We clean and save** all the foam trays from packaged meats and bakery items. When our melons start setting, I punch two holes in the trays for drainage and slip a tray under each melon. This keeps the melons clean and makes them easier to find.     —*Thelma Carpenter*
*Great Bend, Kansas*

**To prolong** our harvest, I plant several varieties of early, mid-season and late peppers and tomatoes.
—*Sue Gronholz*
*Columbus, Wisconsin*

**When my tomatoes** start blooming, I sprinkle flour on the blossoms to help them set. Since I've been doing this, I've been getting more tomatoes.  —*Oma Dell Burch*
*Medina, Texas*

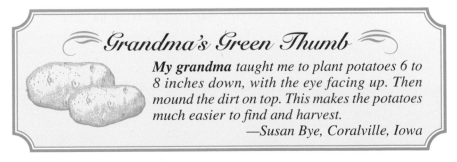

## Grandma's Green Thumb

**My grandma** taught me to plant potatoes 6 to 8 inches down, with the eye facing up. Then mound the dirt on top. This makes the potatoes much easier to find and harvest.
—*Susan Bye, Coralville, Iowa*

# CHAPTER EIGHT

# THE SPICE OF LIFE

A PINCH OF THIS and a dash of that...why not add a little spice to your garden by planting some herbs? They'll offer texture and fragrance in your garden and season your meals, too.

We've grouped these ideas and hints for growing herbs and spices thanks to a suggestion from gardeners Kimberly and Keri Nelson of State College, Pennsylvania.

"Growing herbs certainly spiced up our life," they wrote. "Why not include a chapter called 'Spice of Life'?" So we did.

**Our yard is small**, so I grow basil and oregano in pots on the patio. They're handy whenever I want to snip a few sprigs to add to my pasta sauce. When the weather gets cold, I bring the pots inside and enjoy fresh herbs all winter.

—*Linda Famous*
*Boyertown, Pennsylvania*

**Garlic** is easy to grow. Find a sunny spot to plant the cloves. It multiplies and also forms seeds, which should be left to dry on the stalk before harvesting.

—*Marsha Melder*
*Shreveport, Louisiana*

**Here's a trick** to keep invasive herbs, like mint, from taking over your garden. Cut holes in the bottom of a large plastic pot—the kind you get from nurseries when you buy a tree or shrub. Bury the pot in your garden with the rim sticking above the soil. Then fill the pot with soil and plant the sprigs of mint inside the pot. I've grown mint in my garden this way for two seasons and so far none of it has "escaped".

—*Susan Tyndall*
*Deep Run, North Carolina*

**I chop my herbs**, such as basil, oregano, dill and tarragon, in my food processor. Then I put them in ice cube trays with water and freeze them. After the cubes are frozen, I store them in labeled bags in the freezer and then just pop them into stews and sauces when needed.

—*Joan Amato*
*Downsville, New York*

**Visitors enjoy** our unusual herbs, like the "Vicks plant" (*Plectranthus purpuratus*), which smells just like Vicks Vap-O-Rub. This tender perennial falls gracefully from hanging baskets and must be brought indoors for winter.

—*Toye Spence, Baker City, Oregon*

**Boxed herbal teas** can be quite expensive. Growing your own is a good alternative. Mint for teas is very easy to grow. I store the dried crushed leaves in an airtight container and "brew" the tea in a drip coffee maker. It's "tea-licious"!

—*Deborah Moyer*
*Liberty, Pennsylvania*

**My dried herbs** are as colorful as the fresh ones. (I hate brown parsley!) I put freshly snipped herbs in a brown paper lunch bag, close with a paper clip and punch four holes in the bag with the tines of a fork. Then I put the bag in the refrigerator. Each morning, I give it a shake and turn it over. When the herbs are completely dry, I simply store them until they're needed.

—*Helen Maurer*
*Elmhurst, Illinois*

**For a longer** herb harvest, I plant the same varieties at 2-week intervals. This also works for lettuce, spinach and radishes.

—*Sue Gronholz*
*Columbus, Wisconsin*

**To entice** butterflies and bees to your garden, plant oregano, borage, catnip and hollyhocks.
—*Ardith Morton*
*Merriman, Nebraska*

**Here's an easy way** to grow herbs in areas that have cold winters. Plant the herbs in pots and sink them into the ground in spring. Harvest them through the summer. Then dig up the pots before frost and keep them growing indoors.
—*Verna Fairley, Hillsboro, Ohio*

**I hang up** parsley, basil, oregano, etc., to completely dry. Then I store them in airtight jars so I always have fresh herbs on hand.
—*Elaine Doyle*
*Onalaska, Wisconsin*

**I dry herbs** in paper bags, then put a variety in a nice bottle, fill with oil and cap. Add a ribbon and card, and you have a lovely home-grown gift. —*Elizabeth Srutowski*
*Mesa, Arizona*

**I harvest** basil, oregano, parsley, cilantro and thyme frequently with scissors. Then I water, fertilize and watch for other cuttings until frost. I wash them well, trim any unwanted stems, then bag and freeze them. They darken a bit, but they retain their wonderful full-strength flavor, and they can be chopped straight from the freezer. —*Sharon Scholz*
*Oakland, Oregon*

**If you want to grow** herbs but are short on space, try a strawberry jar. It's portable and can be moved to a sunny spot indoors for the winter. I've used this method for thyme, mint, oregano, basil, chives, burnet, parsley and marjoram. Keep the potting soil moist but not wet.
—*Charlene Margetiak*
*Norwalk, Ohio*

**Pennyroyal** (careful, it can be a weedy and aggressive plant) was the sovereign insecticide of pioneer days. Start a bed of it, then plant sprigs in garden rows that are most susceptible to insects. When ants invaded my okra, I draped pennyroyal sprigs among the blooms and pods, and that stopped the pests.
—*Dovie Owens, Fulton, Mississippi*

## *Grandma's Green Thumb*

**Grandma protected** her family from mosquito bites by planting lemon balm or pennyroyal in the garden, or in pots near the door. Just pull off a stem and rub it on your skin or clothes, and the mosquitoes won't bite. —*Toye Spence*
*Baker City, Oregon*

# CHAPTER NINE

# FROM THE GROUND UP: LAWNS TO TREES

FROM UNDER YOUR FEET to over your head, the grass, shrubs and trees not only make our backyards more interesting, they also give wild birds and other backyard critters food and shelter.

Here is a handful of reader tips to make your lawns look like carpets and to turn your landscaping plants into a beautiful backdrop for your backyard activities.

**In addition** to regular fertilizing and overseeding in fall, our biggest secret for a lush lawn is keeping the mower at the highest setting. The tall grass looks strange at first, but it helps the lawn survive hot weather. When everyone else's grass is drying up, ours stays green with no other maintenance.

—*Katie Vandergriff*
*Powell, Tennessee*

**Here's a trick** to rid your yard and flower beds of creeping-Charlie (also called ground ivy). When the weed's leaves are rain-soaked or heavy with dew, sprinkle them carefully with dry 20-Mule Team Borax. This will kill them. Be accurate so you do not sprinkle the borax on turf or flowers, which could also be damaged by this treatment.

—*Lucille Van Dyke*
*Grinnell, Iowa*

**When transplanting** a tree, attach a twist-tie or nylon to a branch on one side of the tree (I always choose the east side). Then when you re-plant the tree, you can place it in the same direction so it continues to receive the same exposure to the sun. —*Joellen Batten-Siebers*
*Moose Lake, Minnesota*

**Here's how** to start a dogwood tree from seed:

• Pick the seeds when fully ripe. (Watch the birds, they'll feast on them when ripe.)

• Peel the red skin and pulp off each seed (they're about the size of a grain of rice).

• Wet some peat moss and squeeze out the excess moisture.

• Put the seeds in the damp moss, cover with a plastic bag and seal with a twist-tie.

• Place in a refrigerator vegetable bin for 6 months.

• Carefully open in spring (some seeds may have already begun to

**To slowly** and gently water your newly planted trees with minimal run off, take a 5-gallon plastic bucket and drill a small hole at the bottom. Place the bucket near the trunk and fill with water. It will drip slowly, helping the water get to the tree's roots.

—*Mrs. Gregory Krehbiel*
*Moundridge, Kansas*

sprout) and plant each seed 1/2 inches deep in its own container with good potting soil.

• Set in a warm place and keep moist. In a few days you will see your little tree begin to sprout.

*—Jane Woodson*
*Auburn, California*

**My apples**, cherries and pears were always spotted and bug-damaged even though I sprayed them. Last year, I tried soaking a pack of chewing tobacco in 3 gallons of water, then spraying. (Leftover tobacco tea is toxic and should be kept away from children and pets.) It really made a difference. I sprayed weekly and right after rains until the fruit was well-formed.

*—Myron Minnich*
*Lewistown, Ohio*

**I've finally** come up with a way to reseed the spots on my lawn where my golden retrievers love to roll. I seed the areas and then lay chicken wire over the patches. The dogs avoid them, and the sun and water can get through it.

*—Maureen Conroy FitzGerald*
*Oak Park, Illinois*

**To keep** small critters and insects out of your yard, mix 1/4 cup Dawn dishwashing liquid with water in a bottle that attaches to your garden hose, then spray the lawn. Make sure you don't spray ornamental plants. *—Lynn Hart*
*Jacksonville, Florida*

**Don't collect grass** clippings when you mow your lawn. Mow often enough so that the clippings aren't too long and then leave them to fertilize the lawn. Also, if you're creating a garden in a lawn area, don't throw away the grass that needs to be removed. Use it to patch bare spots in your lawn.

*—Marsha Melder*
*Shreveport, Louisiana*

**When our** favorite maple tree died, I didn't want to cut it down, so we planted lots of morning glories around it. It's about 25 feet tall, and the vines would grow even taller if they had somewhere to go.

*—Barb Gallow*
*Neenah, Wisconsin*

**After picking up** black walnuts or husking them, I use a cut green tomato to remove the stains from my hands. It's worked for me for years. *—Ella Eshenbaugh*
*Freeport, Pennsylvania*

**Our lawn** had bare patches, so I applied a thin layer of chicken manure in late fall. The next summer, our lawn was like velvet. My husband had to mow it twice a week.

*—Carolyn McGuire*
*Rumford, Maine*

**To avoid** a striped lawn when fertilizing, use a half-strength setting and spread the entire yard in one direction. Then repeat, again at half strength, perpendicular to the first application. *—Sharon Jensen*
*Dubuque, Iowa*

**In fall**, feed your lawn with winter fertilizer. I do this between mid-October and mid-November. Also spread lime in acid soils to ensure that all the fertilizer is available to plants. —*John Vrabely*
*Linden, New Jersey*

**To start** new yews, just plant pruned clippings in the ground, then set glass jars over them until rooted. (Watch closely so the plants don't overheat.) In a year, you'll have all the shrubs you want.
—*Jacob Fisher*
*Quarryville, Pennsylvania*

**Azaleas are known** for promptly dying after being transplanted. Here's how to successfully transplant one.

Gently slide the plant out of its original container. Then use an old fork, screwdriver or other pointed instrument to rough up the entire surface of the tangled root ball, including the bottom. Do a thorough job and don't be alarmed if some of the roots break off. If you fail to do this step, the roots will remain in a ball, they will not grow outward and the plant will die.

Next, dunk the entire plant—leaves, roots and all—into a bucket of water. It may float at first, but by holding it in the water, the root ball will begin to saturate and eventually sink. Leave the plant in the water until no more bubbles rise from the root ball. The root ball must be wet to the core before transplanting.

The plant can safely be left in the water for several hours. Then plant it in an appropriate place where it will reward you with vigorous growth. —*Della Runyan*
*Santa Rose, California*

**When you sow** grass seed, add ordinary flour to it so that the area is "whitened". This will help you easily find where it was planted.
—*Mrs. James Grisdale*
*Mount Pleasant, Michigan*

**Use all-purpose flour** to mark the places where you want to plant trees and shrubs. That way, the spacing remains just as you planned, even if the containers need to be moved while digging.
—*Carole Bergman*
*Anderson, South Carolina*

**Save your** discarded Christmas tree for the birds. Just tie it around feeder posts or tree trunks near feed-

**To keep deer** from trees and plants, place tall stakes around them and wrap with hardware cloth or snow fencing for a protective barrier.
—*Cathie Huguenin*
*Stevensville, Montana*

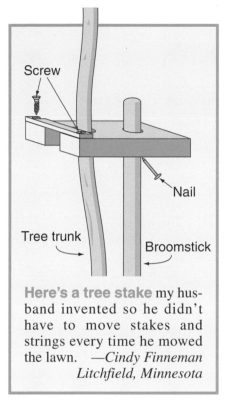

**Here's a tree stake** my husband invented so he didn't have to move stakes and strings every time he mowed the lawn.  —*Cindy Finneman
Litchfield, Minnesota*

the design. Plus, we're sure we can easily mow around the area once it's planted.

Then we add a 1/4-inch-thick layer of newspaper on the uncut grass. We cover it with 8 to 10 inches of topsoil and wet it down. To plant annuals and perennials, pierce the newspaper to make sure the roots can spread easily.—*Astrid Belanger
Columbia, Connecticut*

**To kill thistles** in your yard, sprinkle a little table salt in the center of the thistle. It works best on warm sunny days. If done in the morning, the weeds will be dead by nightfall. (Be careful to apply only to the plant so you don't damage the soil for other desirable plants.)  —*Joy Westphal
Pecatonica, Illinois*

ers. The birds will love the extra shelter.  —*Eldora Zimmerman
Durand, Illinois*

**Use large coffee cans** with the top and bottom cut off to protect little bushes and trees from lawn mowers. Be sure to remove them as the trunks get larger.
—*Cathie Huguenin
Stevensville, Montana*

**Years ago**, we discovered a unique method of building a garden.

After choosing a site, we let the grass grow until it's ready for its next mowing. Then we use a lawn mower to outline the shape of the bed. This makes it easy to visualize

**I create** "living" backyard sculptures that resemble animals, including bears, dolphins, penguins and even dinosaurs. The only tools needed are needle-nose pliers, gloves and a long-sleeved shirt to turn chicken wire fencing into these works of art.

After bending and cutting, the creatures begin to take shape. But to finish the masterpieces, I plant an evergreen yew bush within each creation.

As the bush begins to grow within the wire frame, I use hand clippers to prune the shrubs into the desired shape. Within a few years, the "animals" fill out and I just trim them as needed.  —*Hersel Kile
Council Bluffs, Iowa*

# CHAPTER TEN

# 'A PILE OF GOLD'

IF SOMEONE calls your compost pile a "really rottin' idea", be sure to thank them.

Adding compost made from yard and kitchen waste is one of the easiest and most inexpensive ways to improve your soil. As they say, great gardens start from the ground up!

With a little attention and time (turning the pile with a garden fork every once in a while will speed up the process), you'll soon have beautiful "black gold".

**Every fall** I put three to four wheel-barrows full of leaves into an open compost bin and add a little soil. By the next growing season, I have a wheelbarrow full of black soil.
—*Inga Burkholder*
*Cecil Lake, British Columbia*

**One of the best hints** for creating compost quickly is to reduce the size of the material. The bigger it is, the longer it takes to decompose. Use a lawn mower or shredder to break down garden waste or leaves whenever possible. Turning the pile once a week keeps air circulating, which also speeds up decomposition.
—*Joseph Novara*
*Kalamazoo, Michigan*

**I collect kitchen** scraps in a Tupperware canister. When it's full, I take it outside, dig a hole and bury the scraps. In a few weeks, it turns to "black gold". The next time I pick a different spot. This saves a lot of time and work.
—*Evelyn Shanken*
*Murrieta, California*

**Put two or three layers** of newspapers on your flower beds, cover with your usual mulch and water. This will last a season or two. As a bonus, the earthworms eat the paper, and you'll have more of them in your garden.
—*Rose Fischer*
*Chesapeake, Virginia*

**I put fruit** and vegetable peelings into my blender instead of a compost pile. Then I dig a hole in my garden, pour in the mixture and cover the hole. It saves me from hav-ing to find a place for a compost pile.
—*Virginia Moye*
*New Oxford, Pennsylvania*

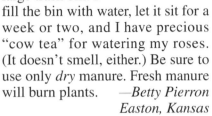

**I collect** well-dried cow manure from our pasture and put a shovel-ful or two in a large trash bin. I fill the bin with water, let it sit for a week or two, and I have precious "cow tea" for watering my roses. (It doesn't smell, either.) Be sure to use only *dry* manure. Fresh manure will burn plants.
—*Betty Pierron*
*Easton, Kansas*

**I use grass clippings** in my three compost piles. (Avoid using clippings from lawns with invasive grasses or recently treated with weed killers.) I put fresh clippings on one pile the first week, then move them to the second pile the second week and then to the last pile the third week. By then the clippings are ready to use in the garden. I continue this rotation to keep the cycle going all summer. A lattice fence hides the piles from view.
—*Albert Percle Sr., Sargent, Texas*

**This is the simplest** composting method I know. We keep a compost bucket outside the back door. As often as necessary, we empty it into a trench and cover with soil. I give my daughters a penny for every worm they find at the creek, and then I put the worms on top of the trench.
—*Janet Christoph*
*Mebane, North Carolina*

**I make special holders** for my compost so my plants receive a drink of "compost tea" whenever it rains. I bury vegetable cans that have holes punched in the bottom in the ground near the plant. Then I cut the bottoms out of plastic milk jugs and place those upside-down in the sunken tin cans.

I fill the milk jugs with compost from our pile. When it rains or when you water, the compost produces a "tea", which drains down into the can, out the holes in the bottom and into the soil near the plant's roots.

This method also works well for growing cantaloupes. I put the compost jug in the can on a mounded pile of garden soil. Then I plant the cantaloupe seeds around the compost jug.  —*Naomi Ochs Independence, Missouri*

**"Sheet composting"** works well in central Florida where the soil is almost 100% sand. It's so warm here, with an average annual rainfall of over 50 inches, that there's no need for a compost pile. So, I spread the material directly on the soil. If there's a lot, I run the tiller through the garden to mix it into the soil. It's taken about 8 years, but my soil is nice and dark now.
 —*Chris Stephan, Sebring, Florida*

**I built** a compost bin at the end of my small garden. Then I asked a neighbor to empty his lawn mower bag into it whenever he mows. I put my own clippings in the bin, too.
 —*Yoli Quevedo Anacortes, Washington*

**I make compost** in a heavy plastic trash can with wheels and a lockdown lid. It's lightweight, mobile and retains moisture. Several holes drilled about 7 inches apart near the top of the can provide aeration.
 —*Beverly Howell Montrose, Colorado*

**The key** to successful compost is using no meat products and cutting fruit and vegetable items into very small pieces. When babies take smaller bites, they digest their food better. It's the same for compost!
 —*Barbara Eddy Rio Rancho, New Mexico*

**I put peat moss** in the bottom of my chicken house for the hens to dust in during rainy periods. The peat stays dry, and when the chick-

ens dust and scratch in the hen-house, they keep the droppings stirred and dry. The peat and chicken droppings cleaned from the hen-house can go directly into my vegetable garden and flower beds in fall, so it can age until spring. (The mixture must age so it doesn't burn your plants.)  —*Linda Becker*
*Olympia, Washington*

**Got a favorite** flower patch whose soil needs enriching? Know a place where fishermen buy worms? Bring home that rich black dirt and a bunch of worms and sprinkle them into the "problem patch". After one season, even the most problematic soils will be enriched, aerated and producing healthy flowers.
—*Gerald McLaughlin*
*New Castle, Pennsylvania*

**My son-in-law** came up with a plan for an inexpensive composting bin. Secure four wooden pallets with bungee cords to form a square. Use two cords on three of the corners, and one on the fourth. When I want to turn the pile, I remove the cord from the fourth corner to open the swing-out "gate" and get to work with my pitchfork.
—*Betty Dusicsko*
*Fairview, Pennsylvania*

**Rake or "mow"** fallen leaves and pack them into plastic leaf bags that you've poked holes in. Water the leaves thoroughly and tie the tops of the bags. The alternate freeze-thaw cycles of our normal Montana winters break down the leaves into

---

## WORDS TO GROW BY

**Scatter lawn clippings** of non-invasive grasses around flower and vegetable plants to keep your gardens lush, even during dry spells. This will hold moisture in and keep weeds down. It also puts nutrients back in the soil.
—*Nancy Rivers*
*Sheridan, Illinois*

---

beautiful loamy black soil for gardens or planters.
—*Mrs. A.C. Wallace*
*Billings, Montana*

**I use compost** to help keep my rose garden free of weeds. After weeding, I lay several layers of newspaper down over the area, wet them down and then cover them with compost. This combination keeps the weeds from sprouting, and the paper eventually breaks down and benefits the soil.
—*Elvera Darmer*
*Andover, Minnesota*

**I make** lots of compost, but I really don't have an exact recipe. I use some green materials, some dry materials, a few kitchen scraps and a little manure. Just turn the pile every week or two, and soon it'll be ready to use. And remember...*never* add diseased plants to the pile.
—*Sue Gronholz*
*Columbus, Wisconsin*

**It's said** that a few branches of yarrow will help a compost pile "mature" faster.

*—Crystal White*
*Chesterton, Indiana*

**Putting lime** between layers "sweetens" my compost pile and prevents odors. I also shake dry Miracle-Gro fertilizer between layers to speed decomposition. I never cover the pile or rake it, and it's emptied only in spring. Larger pieces go back to the pile, and we start all over with grass clippings, trimmings from spring cleanup, etc. I have beautiful healthy compost with little or no work.

*—Judy Farris*
*Toledo, Ohio*

**Nothing goes to waste** in our garden. Rotten and critter-damaged vegetables go into our compost bin. In fall, I run stalks, vines and foliage through our chipper-shredder for mulch. After the holidays, I lay branches from discarded Christmas trees over the garden. By late March, some of the needles have already decayed into the soil.

*—Mickey Hamilton*
*Gilbertsville, Pennsylvania*

**We use** our kitchen waste (vegetables only—no meat or dairy products) and garden waste for compost. I never turn it; I just add a little sand to the pile occasionally. The secret is cutting stalks and other large items into pieces no larger than 2 inches.

*—Helen Zeh*
*Cohocton, New York*

**I improved** poor garden soil by covering it with all the grass clippings I could get my hands on. (Avoid using clippings from lawns with invasive grasses or recently treated with weed killers.) I went to a pasture and scooped up cow patties to throw on, too. The following spring, I could grow just about anything in that soil.

*—L.D. Aplin Jr.*
*Greenville, Texas*

**Whenever I have** fruit or potato peelings, strawberry tops, eggshells, even coffee grounds, I put them in my blender with a little water. Then I dump the ground particles on the garden and water thoroughly. My relatives marvel at the results I've gotten.

*—Marna Hodson*
*Scottsburg, Indiana*

**Smelly compost?** Just add leaves or other dry materials to the pile. Then turn it in. The materials will help dry out the pile and eliminate the smell.

*—Melinda Myers*
*Milwaukee, Wisconsin*

**Wrap 10 feet** of chicken wire around 4 stakes to make a three-sided compost bin. Pile grass clippings 5 to 6 inches deep, spread on a handful of Ringer's Compost, a bacteria powder that speeds decomposition, and water well. Repeat whenever you add garden or vegetable waste to the pile.

When you have two or more layers, turn the pile with a pitchfork. If the smell is bad, you may need to turn the pile more often. At the end of the growing season, cover with plastic until early spring.

—*John Vrabely*
*Linden, New Jersey*

**I make furniture** from rough timbers and put most of the wood chips and sawdust in the compost pile. I use my tiller to stir the mixture into the garden once it is completely decomposed. It does a first-class job of improving the soil. (Don't mix wood products directly into garden soil. There will be a lack of nitrogen, which will stunt plant growth.)

—*Willard Bedwell*
*Maryville, Tennessee*

**We raise cattle** and have found their manure really helps our gardens. We let it dry in a sunny area and combine it with cornstalks and a little soil. When the mixture is dry, we store it in containers. Then we sprinkle it on beds and rake it into the soil.

—*Krystal Norris*
*Bedford, Iowa*

**The soil** where we live in central New Jersey has a lot of clay. We make our own compost to add to the soil, but I've found something else that's helpful. After eating pistachios, we throw the shells directly into the garden. They seem to aerate the clay soil and prevent it from becoming too hard.

—*Raymond Drewniany*
*Roselle, New Jersey*

**Perk up your perennials** with a drink of compost tea. Fill a burlap

**Don't throw away** coffee grounds. They are biodegradable and excellent for your gardens and flower beds. I dry them and sprinkle them over my flowers—even on top of the snow in winter. They will get to the ground eventually. They add a little acid to the soil, which is especially good for azaleas. And worms love 'em, too!   —*Sondra Boyd*
*Shelby, Ohio*

sack or a large square of cheesecloth half-full with compost. Tie the top with a string and soak it for a week in a large covered container of water. Remove the sack and use the "tea" that remains as liquid fertilizer.   —*Angela Griffin Hatchett*
*Altoona, Alabama*

**Instead of raking** leaves, use your lawn mower with a bagger to pick them up. This chops them into fine pieces and makes excellent mulch for the garden.

—*Mary Ann Graber*
*Bloomfield, Indiana*

**Every fall**, after I clean the garden out, I put on a lot of compost and till it into the soil.

—*Lawrence Gostomski*
*Thorp, Wisconsin*

**Here's my basic recipe** for making compost in a tumbler (a 55-gallon drum that can be rotated to turn the materials).

Fill the tumbler with equal weights of grass clippings and leaves, saving enough space at the opening to put in 6 shovels full of composted manure, 6 shovels full of sawdust and any green food plant waste (no meats or dairy products). Be sure not to include weeds.

Run water on the pile for 1 minute and let materials drain. If turned several times each day, your material will be very fine and ready within weeks.

Apply water as needed into the compost pile while materials are breaking down, but don't soak your pile. It should be no wetter than a damp sponge. —*Marie Musser*
*Hildale, Utah*

**Use your blender** to grind up vegetable and fruit peelings, pulp, etc. Adding this to your compost pile will give it diversity and moisture. Liquefied scraps break down faster and are assimilated into the compost more quickly.

—*Beverly Howell*
*Montrose, Colorado*

**I scatter** bedding straw on the floor of my chicken house. My chickens like to scratch and scatter it about as they look for bits of food.

When the straw becomes full of chicken droppings, I remove it and pile it outside. I leave it there all winter to decompose.

When it's time to prepare the garden soil, I spread this processed manure and straw on the soil and work it in. —*Clara Belle Tye*
*Washougal, Washington*

**A kitty** litter sifting set is the perfect tool for sifting the organic material from your compost pile before you add it to your garden.

The set includes a plastic sifter pan and one or two bottom pans. Just put compost in the sifter pan, and in a matter of seconds, the smaller pieces fall through to the bottom pan. The pieces that are too big remain in the sifter and can be returned to the compost pile to finish decomposing.

These sets are easy to handle and store, and they won't rust if left outdoors. Best of all, they're reasonably priced at most department or hardware stores. I bought mine for less than $10.

—*Flavio Gallegos*
*Fort Lyon, Colorado*

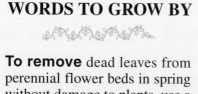

## WORDS TO GROW BY

**To remove** dead leaves from perennial flower beds in spring without damage to plants, use a child's rake to get in among them. —*Alma Hansen*
*New Denmark, New Brunswick*

**I chop all garden waste** (corncobs, vegetable and flower stalks, tomato vines, etc.) and put it in a 12-foot by 3-foot by 30-inch-high compost pit in the corner of my backyard. I throw in kitchen waste (no animal products) and grass clippings free of weed killers, too.

A few times during warm weather, I add a layer of soil and a couple pounds of ordinary lawn fertilizer. Then I water it thoroughly.

Because the pile is so big, I do not "turn" the contents regularly. But I've discovered it "ripens" beautifully in a few years. And there is plenty of rich material to share with neighbors.

*—Mrs. A.C. Wallace*
*Billings, Montana*

**After the first** tilling and weeding of our garden, we use grass clippings as a 3- to 4-inch-thick mulch. (Avoid using clippings from invasive grasses or from lawns recently treated with weed killers.) In fall, the grass is tilled under to improve the soil for next year.

*—Edris Weinand*
*St. Cloud, Minnesota*

**I never have enough** organic material to add to my compost pile. So I go to fruit stands in the area and ask for their overripe fruit. They're going to throw it away anyway, so they're usually happy to get rid of it. And it's free! *—Linda Kovalchick*
*Spokane, Washington*

**I built** my compost bin from used wood pallets. They're often free for the asking at home building centers. Plus, the spaces between the pallet boards allow air to circulate through the material in the bin.

*—Earl Ruby*
*West Hartford, Connecticut*

**The leaves** in your compost pile help the air circulate throughout the heap and provide a good source of carbon. Grass clippings are an excellent source of nitrogen.

Adding equal weights of these materials will make an ideal compost pile. *—Dan McCoy*
*Oostburg, Wisconsin*

**I cover the top** of my compost bin with an old piece of carpet. The materials in the bin should be as moist as a wrung-out sponge. If they're too dry, sprinkle them with a fine mist from your garden hose, but be careful not to make them too wet.

*—Marion King*
*Gloucester, Ontario*

# CHAPTER ELEVEN

# 'THIS MEANS WAR!'

WHILE OUR BACKYARDS may seem like private "outdoor living rooms", most of the time we share them with local wildlife.

Here are some suggestions you may find helpful when you encounter uninvited guests.

Not all of the hints will work in all situations (for example, scare tactics do not work as well in urban areas because these critters are used to a lot of activity), but hopefully there is an idea or two that may work in your backyard.

No matter which tactic you use, don't forget to monitor its effectiveness throughout the growing season. If one method stops working, odds are your guests have become accustomed to your deterrent. In other words...you'll have to move on to "Plan B".

**When all else failed** to keep deer out of my garden at night, I bought a security light with two sockets and a 4-second "test" setting. I plugged a lightbulb in one socket and a radio tuned to a 24-hour station in the other. When the motion detector senses movement, both the light and radio come on at the same time. I doubt that deer know the power is on for only 4 seconds because they're probably in the next county by then. —*Joe Mahoney*
*La Grange, Georgia*

**If deer are feasting** on your trees, break a bar of Ivory soap into several pieces and hang them from strings on the tree. I also sprinkle soap around tulips if the deer are eating them. This works really well.
—*Amy Wolfe*
*Kittanning, Pennsylvania*

**For years**, my crocuses, tulips and pansies succumbed to the appetites of chipmunks and rabbits. I tried mothballs and hot red pepper, but no luck. Blood meal turned out to be the answer. It not only repels critters, but is a fine fertilizer as well. —*Fran Byron*
*Ellicott City, Maryland*

**I put Irish Spring** soap in nylon anklets and attach the socks to sticks in each corner of my garden. A white plastic bag flies atop a fifth stick. (White signals danger to white-tailed deer.) It works—I've seen deer stand in the adjacent empty plot and turn their noses up at my garden. —*Mildred Carlson*
*Gilby, North Dakota*

**If deer like to nibble** on your roses and shrubs, try this recipe to keep them away. Beat 12 to 18 eggs in a blender, then mix with 5 gallons of water. Spray the liquid on plants (except those with fruits or vegetables that you plan to eat), reapplying after any heavy rains.
—*Sandy Miller, Toledo, Washington*

**I tried everything** to keep deer out of my perennial beds, but nothing worked until I discovered a product called Hinder. I sprayed it faithfully every week and after heavy rains. Since then I haven't had any problems with deer. My gardens never looked more beautiful.
—*Denise Connolly*
*Smallwood, New York*

**Want to keep deer away?** Fill a No. 2 coffee can halfway with wheat flour, add about 1-1/2 ounces of black pepper and mix. Punch holes in the can lid and shake the mixture over your plants when dew is on them or after a rain. The deer might eat your plants *once*, but they won't return for days. I have no problem all summer when I use this method.
—*L.O. Kuper, Council Bluffs, Iowa*

Some flowers, herbs and shrubs will survive visits from deer. They include daffodils, most daisies, gaillardia, coreopsis, asters, primula, California poppies, iris, lily of the valley, St. John's wort, barberry, valerian, lavender, oregano, mint, garlic, rosemary, butterfly bush, holly, ferns, English ivy, bamboo, japonica, heather, pennyroyal, foxglove and chamomile.
—*Marj Trim, Sooke, British Columbia*

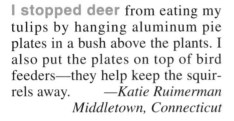

I stopped deer from eating my tulips by hanging aluminum pie plates in a bush above the plants. I also put the plates on top of bird feeders—they help keep the squirrels away. —*Katie Ruimerman Middletown, Connecticut*

Spring Hill, a mail-order nursery, advises planting marigolds and boxwoods to repel deer. Deer also avoid Colorado spruce, barberry, holly, lamb's ear and Siberian iris, as well as some ferns, ornamental grasses and ground covers. —*Lora Schreiber West Bend, Wisconsin*

Deer were visiting our garden every night until we bought an electronic device that emits a high-frequency sound audible only to animals. They must not like it much— it keeps deer out most of the time.
—*Marilyn Ball, Hudson, Ohio*

After losing lots of plants to deer, we set steel fence posts around our garden and strung bird netting between the posts. It worked! Since it's see-through, we enjoy our beautiful garden without the intrusions of our "deer friends" or the ugly sight of a heavy fence. —*Karen Case Greendale, Wisconsin*

Neighborhood cats were using my garden as a litter box. Then I put branches trimmed from my cedar tree around my plants. It worked…no more broken or dug-up plants. —*Irene Romanofsky Gardner, Illinois*

To discourage deer from munching on young apple and maple trees, tie white plastic bags to some of the branches. Perhaps the bags look like white tails—the deer's "warning system". Also, the bags are visible on moonlit nights and rustle in the breeze. Whatever the reasons, the bags work. —*Jean Jungst Garfield, Minnesota*

**To discourage** hungry deer, raccoons and rabbits from snacking on my garden, I plant a "flower fence" around it. I put cannas very thickly on three sides and use marigolds on the fourth.　　　—*Doris Gish*
*Remer, Minnesota*

**To keep deer** from eating new trees, hang wind chimes in the branches or lay chicken wire on the ground around the trunks.
—*Margaret Lindow*
*Suamico, Wisconsin*

**After years** of deer and dog damage, I now plant my lilies, roses and petunias in large containers. We drilled holes in empty 15-gallon tubs and added 4 inches of gravel before putting in the garden soil.
—*Gloria Porter*
*Grandin, North Dakota*

**I sprinkle** Milorganite 6-2-0 fertilizer around my flowers every week and after it rains. This not only feeds the plants, it keeps deer away, too. In winter, I put 2 tablespoons in small bags and hang them on rhododendrons and mountain laurels so deer won't eat the leaves.
—*Nancy Terwilliger*
*Butler, Pennsylvania*

**To keep** deer away, sprinkle your garden with a mixture of crushed garlic, garlic powder and dill pickle juice. Your neighbors will think you're cooking spaghetti—and so will the deer. They don't care for the smell.　　　—*Jen Wood*
*Newfane, Vermont*

**Decomposed** horse manure is an effective deer repellent around flowers and bushes. Any place that boards horses probably will give you the stuff free. We've also had some success in keeping deer away by alternating baby powder, Dog-Off, mothballs (keep mothballs away from kids and pets) and shavings of Irish Spring soap.
—*Bernard and Joan Timmer*
*Paris, Michigan*

**An electric fence** keeps deer and raccoons out of my corn. I also use chicken wire to keep rabbits away from my bean sprouts.
—*Irene Jones, Chardon, Ohio*

**To keep deer** and small animals from eating my sweet corn, I put a three strand electric fence around the garden. The lowest wire is 6 inches from the ground. The second wire is 12 inches above the ground, and the top wire is about waist high. I haven't had problems with critters for years.
—*Joseph Wantz*
*Union Bridge, Maryland*

**This mixture** will keep rabbits from eating flowers and shrubs. Blend or whisk together 1 tablespoon castor oil, 2 tablespoons liquid dish soap and 6 tablespoons water. Dilute 1 tablespoon of mixture per 1 gallon of water and pour over plants. Reapply after each rain.
—*Audrey DeSimone*
*Montgomery City, Missouri*

**We've tried** everything to keep the deer from our gardens. So far, the only thing that has worked is blood meal fertilizer.

I use coffee filters with 1/4 cup or more of blood meal in each filter. I pull the edges together to form a bag and staple. Then I push a wire through the stapled area and attach it to a plant. I replace as needed.

*—Barbara Martin*
*Coarsegold, California*

**If the deer** are eating your evergreens, or leaf-eating insects are devouring your veggies, try this homemade repellent.

Place five garlic cloves, one onion and three red-hot chili peppers in a blender with a quart of water. Then liquefy. Allow the mix to sit overnight and strain. Add 1/4 cup of dishwashing soap to the mix and pour into a spray bottle to spray on your plants. *—Donald Henkel*
*Duluth, Minnesota*

**To keep deer** from flowers and shrubs, add one or two raw eggs to a gallon of water and stir. Then spray the mixture on the plants. The egg solution will rot. It will go unnoticed by humans but not by deer. (Do not use raw egg mixes on vegetable plants.) *—Ced Vig*
*Rhinelander, Wisconsin*

**Put human hair** clippings around the border of your garden to discourage deer and raccoons.

*—Patricia Dobbs*
*Ferryville, Wisconsin*

**When stray cats** began using my flower beds as "comfort stations", I cut some long thorny branches off my climbing roses and laid them along the middle of the beds. Problem solved!

*— Opal Kuhns*
*Grand Junction, Colorado*

**My cat thought** I planted impatiens just for her to sleep on. So I placed pinecones and spiny fruit balls from sweet gum trees among the plants. They look nice and make for prickly kitty-sitting.

*—Pat Cartwright*
*Kansas City, Missouri*

**Rabbits eating your lettuce?** Birds pecking your tomatoes? Dust the vegetables with talcum powder, and they won't bother them. Of course, you should wash the vegetables well before eating them.

*—Pat Nelson*
*Hammond, Illinois*

**Rabbits will think** a hose circling your garden is a snake and will refuse to cross it. We've done this for many years and have never had a rabbit problem. Make sure you move the hose occasionally.

*—Bonnie Neuberger*
*Lake Benton, Minnesota*

**A tent of chicken wire** will keep rabbits from eating your vegetables. You can make one long enough to cover a whole row. *—Mary Mahn*
*Ravenna, Michigan*

**Clippings** from my dog-grooming business have kept a client's garden rabbit-free for years. He also hangs sacks of dog hair in seedling fruit trees to keep deer from destroying them. Another client spreads dog hair around her yard in spring so the birds can use it for nest building. —*Paula Alfonsi, Almont, Michigan*

**A friend planted chives** around her lilies to keep rabbits away. It works—and you can eat the chives, too! —*Leah Lee, Eastport, Maine*

**Sprinkle lime** on beans and other plants that rabbits eat (except in alkaline or "sweet" soils). It seems to keep beetles off, too. You'll need to repeat after every rain.
—*Madelyn Kinkade*
*Lake Milton, Ohio*

**I keep hungry rabbits** at bay by wrapping tomato cages with chicken wire. Just wrap the wire around a cage, snip it to the desired size and twist loose ends around the cage to hold it in place. Then place the covered cage over the plants that need protection. —*Esther Rayburn*
*Athens, Michigan*

**We keep rabbits**, woodchucks, raccoons and other critters away with a recipe we call "Old Stinky". In a 3-quart jar, mix 3 raw eggs (shells and all) and half a bottle of hot sauce. Fill the container three-quarters full with water. Shake and cap tightly. Ferment for 5 days be fore drizzling around the perimeter of the flower garden. The results are amazing. —*Joan Johnston*
*Milford, Michigan*

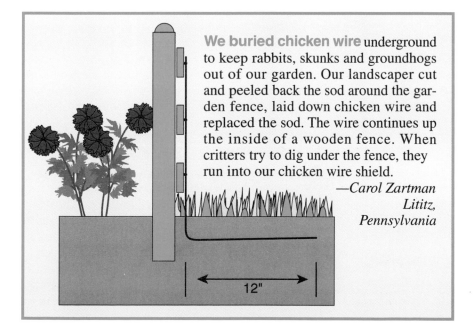

**We buried chicken wire** underground to keep rabbits, skunks and groundhogs out of our garden. Our landscaper cut and peeled back the sod around the garden fence, laid down chicken wire and replaced the sod. The wire continues up the inside of a wooden fence. When critters try to dig under the fence, they run into our chicken wire shield.
—*Carol Zartman*
*Lititz,*
*Pennsylvania*

12"

**After years** of losing my lettuce to rabbits and woodchucks, I finally hit upon a solution. I worked compost into a small patch next to the back-door, then built a simple wooden cold frame to fit it. A plastic lid provides protection from the critters' nocturnal forays.
—*Barbara Dege*
*Hackensack, New Jersey*

**I use large sheer curtains** from thrift shops to keep rabbits and birds from eating my lettuce. I plant lettuce in a patch the size of the curtain, then cover it. Sunshine and rain can still get through. I also use curtains to keep birds from stealing my cherries. Pin or sew several large ones together, throw them over the tree, then pin together around the bottom. The tree won't look pretty, but the method works.
—*Martha Martin*
*Harriston, Ontario*

**We protect** our pepper and tomato plants from rabbits with plastic "tomato baskets" we bought from a neighboring farmer. We cover the plants every night until they either outgrow the baskets or get too big for rabbits to eat. —*Lynn Clark*
*Blenheim, Ontario*

**To keep rabbits** from eating my hostas, I spray the plants with water and then sprinkle the leaves with cayenne pepper. (Wear gloves and do not to touch your eyes when using cayenne pepper.)
—*Helen Braunbach*
*North Tonawanda, New York*

**Chicken wire** made into cylinders and placed around trees and shrubs help keep rabbits away from your plants. —*Cora Rexroad*
*Kingsville, Maryland*

**When raccoons** began raiding my corn, I already had a 3-foot "rabbit guard" fence. So my dad suggested adding a strand of electric livestock fencing around the top since a raccoon climbing the fence would have to grab the electric wire to get over the top. It worked—no more raccoons. —*Sue Gronholz*
*Columbus, Wisconsin*

**To keep raccoons** out of sweet corn, plant pumpkins or squash around the rows. The prickly vines of these plants twined around the cornstalks make the coons think twice before messing with your harvest. I've used this method for years, and I've never lost corn to any critters.
—*Sandy McKenzie*
*Braham, Minnesota*

**After planting my garden**, I border it with clean empty canning jars at 3-foot intervals. The jars reflect light, and the wind whistles over the open tops. I've been doing this for 40 years and have never had a rabbit problem…and we have rabbits everywhere else on our farm.

—*Jan Lindhorst, Burt, Iowa*

**We sprinkle** ashes from our wood burning stove around the garden plants to keep rabbits away. (Use sparingly in alkaline soils, also known as "sweet" soils.)

—*Joan Thomas*
*Springfield, Massachusetts*

**To protect impatiens** from rabbits in early spring, buy a roll of plastic Gutter Guard at the hardware store. Cut to lengths of about 18 inches, form round enclosures for plants and secure with wire ties. Add a screen on top if necessary.

—*Michelene Rocco*
*Lemont, Illinois*

**After grooming** our dog and cats, we place the hair around our newly-planted walnut tree. This keeps rabbits from chewing the bark.

—*Lynda Carpenter*
*Ellsworth, Michigan*

**When rabbits** started eating my statice, I mixed 3 parts water with 1 part of household ammonia and sprayed the ground surrounding my plants. It really has done a good job at discouraging the pests.

—*Nancy Rosengreen*
*Middlefield, Ohio*

**I ask the local** dog groomer for hair clippings. Then I sprinkle them around my transplants. It has worked wonders keeping rabbits away.

—*Darla Friesen*
*Delft, Minnesota*

**To keep** rabbits and cats out of my vegetables and flowers, I sprinkle talcum powder on the ground. For bugs, I spray plants with a mixture of hot pepper sauce, garlic powder and dishwashing liquid. Both remedies must be reapplied after it rains.

—*Violet Glowczynski*
*Calumet City, Illinois*

**My daughter** keeps rabbits out of her garden by digging a trench around the entire garden and filling it with the contents of her vacuum cleaner bag. To keep it from blowing away, she puts screening over it. There is enough scent of humans in this material to frighten off the rabbits.

—*Marlene Eveland*
*St. Thomas, Ontario*

**Squirrels** getting to your bird feeder? Place a 5-foot-tall PVC pipe around your bird feeder pole. Keep the feeder away from anything the squirrels could jump from. Yes, they can climb the pipe—but not if you grease it with cooking oil.

—*Joe Miller, Tallahassee, Florida*

**Many years** ago I was complaining to my neighbor about the rabbits raiding my garden. He suggested scattering glass soft drink bottles around the garden, laying them on their sides.

I don't know if it's the sparkling reflection of the sun or the wind whistling across the openings, but it sure works. The rabbits haven't bothered my garden for 36 years.
—*Barb Sullivan, Rockford, Illinois*

**Dried blood** meal scattered around flowers repels rabbits. Replace after a rain. —*Dorothy Kalinay*
*Van Horne, Iowa*

**To keep** raccoons, squirrels and chipmunks from digging plants out of my outdoor pots, I place prunings from rosebushes on top of the soil. The thornier the branch, the better it works. —*Winifred Linsemier,*
*Galien, Michigan*

**If raccoons and skunks** get into your sweet corn, surround the patch with winter squash or pumpkins. As the vines grow, train them around the outside of the patch so they overlap. This trick has worked for me for years. It's also a convenient way to grow space-consuming vine crops. —*Pat Nelson*
*Cody, Wyoming*

**To keep raccoon** "bandits" out of sweet corn, pour at least an inch of ammonia into a plastic bottle, screw the cap on and punch holes in the bottle above the ammonia. Place one or more bottles around the cornstalks when the ears start showing.
—*Ruth Fehlmahn*
*Tinley Park, Illinois*

**I place small articles** of dirty laundry, like socks, washcloths and T-shirts, on sweet corn stalks a night or two before the ears are ready to pick. The human scent keeps the raccoons away. —*Norma Musser*
*Womelsdorf, Pennsylvania*

**Raccoons always** beat me to my sweet corn until I started surrounding the patch with marigolds, zinnias and cosmos. I also surround my pole beans with these flowers. Once the flowers start blooming, I've noticed both patches also remain virtually insect-free.
—*Roberta Pedrick, Ottumwa, Iowa*

**To keep raccoons** out of your corn patch, sprinkle mothballs in the row. I also put them between cucumbers and melons and don't seem to have as many bugs. (Keep mothballs away from kids and pets.)
—*Lorine Reinhardt, Red Bud, Illinois*

**When our sweet corn** is about ready to pick, we put a radio in the middle of the corn patch to keep raccoons away. We wrap the radio in a clean heavy garbage bag, then tune it to an all-night station. It's the only way we can get any sweet corn for ourselves! —*Ruth Schmerse*
*Janesville, Wisconsin*

**If you're bothered** by raccoons in your corn or watermelon patch, plant two or three pumpkin vines alongside them. The raccoons will leave the other plants alone.  —*Mrs. E.J. Morris Como, Texas*

**We save** our sweet corn from animals by sprinkling pepper on the silks. For larger plots, sprinkle pepper on the silks near the garden edge and on every three to four stalks in the middle. Be sure to reapply the pepper after a rain. —*Lucille Bracy Bluffton, Ohio*

**Garlic helps protect** fruit trees and flowers from animal damage. Plant bulbs beneath trees and throughout beds very early in the spring. When they reseed, extra plants can be pulled, diced and used fresh without waiting for bulbs to form.  —*Barbara Eddy Rio Rancho, New Mexico*

**Attach strips** of red fabric to your tomato cages at the beginning of the season. The birds will grow accustomed to seeing red and won't even pay attention to the fruit when it ripens. —*Ernie and Shawna Landy Valley View, Texas*

**Keep birds out** of your garden and recycle broken VCR tapes at the same time by tying long pieces of the tape to sticks. Then place them around your garden. Birds don't like the shiny fluttering tape.
—*Jennifer Kucera, Tama, Iowa*

**When birds** zoomed in on my ripening tomatoes, I bought three rubber snakes and wound them in the tomato cages. It worked! I also keep birds away by "planting" children's pinwheels throughout the garden.  —*Mary Beth Hall Leander, Texas*

**My Sunday school teacher** keeps birds from her peach tree by placing fake snakes and lizards in it.
—*Eilene Metcalf, Benton, Arkansas*

**I keep birds** out of my tomatoes by putting a clock-radio in a plastic pail, which I set on its side to keep out rain and dew. I'll set the alarm so the radio begins to play in the early morning. This also helps keep animals away, including pesky deer.
—*Grace Anderson Schrunk Blaine, Minnesota*

**My husband** keeps birds from eating his tomatoes by hanging red Christmas ornaments on the plants and fence.

We also fit old pantyhose tops over clusters of green tomatoes. Air and sun can get to them, but the birds can't. They have to do something else—like check out the Christmas ornaments.
—*Van Roberson Houston, Texas*

111

**We protect** our pecan crop from crows and blue jays by tying pieces of cut-up pantyhose around the nut clusters in September.

*—Laurie Gehrt*
*Broken Arrow, Oklahoma*

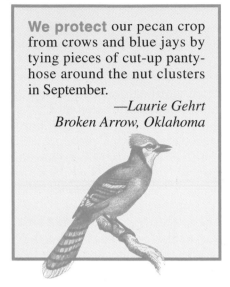

**The birds** ate and pecked at our English peas until we put up a birdbath. Since we installed it 3 years ago, they haven't touched a single pea. Perhaps they were looking for moisture, not food.

*—Florence Black*
*Seminary, Mississippi*

**Five years ago**, we bought a place with a huge population of gophers, moles, voles and shrews. I used a product called Black Leaf from the Wilbur Ellis Co. of Buckner, Kentucky. In 2 weeks, it cleared our 2-1/2 acres of these pests, and we've had no problems since. (Be sure to read and use it according to label directions.)   *—Phil Robinson*
*Weott, California*

**Blackbirds** used to swoop down and break the tops off our new tomato and pepper plants. I stopped them by driving small stakes 10 to 12 feet apart and tying disposable aluminum pie plates on them. If you don't have plates, use large pieces of crumpled foil.   *—Geneva Bias*
*Cedar Lake, Indiana*

**When I get** free compact discs for software advertisements, I make good use of them. I'll tie them in my garden and let the sunlight reflect off them. They make great scarecrows for birds and have even spooked cats.

*—Joyce Chandler-Grigonis*
*Midway Park, North Carolina*

**I hang clean** pull-tab lids from dog-food cans in pairs on our garden fence. The noise scares away the birds—and keeps them from eating the blossoms on my cucumbers.

*—Norine Sejnoha, Cicero, Illinois*

**Our new home** had molehills in the lawn and gophers in the garden. We got rid of both by burying Coke bottles into the ground, leaving about 2 inches sticking out so the wind whistled over the openings.

*—Anna Heinrichs*
*Altona, Manitoba*

**Birds** in your berry patch? Plant native attractants like wild cherry, elderberry and mulberry. The fruits of these trees and shrubs will dull the birds' appetite for your other berries.

*—Ann Ward*
*Naples, Florida*

112

**Recycle old belts** or a piece of garden hose (3 to 4 feet long) by placing them in your garden and around trees. These will scare birds and rabbits that damage your crops because they think it is a snake (move daily). I decorate them with small pieces of colored tape to resemble stripes. —*Rita Chritianson Gleburn, North Dakota*

**We couldn't catch the moles** in our garden with traps, so we opened up their runs, tossed mothballs in either end and closed them back up. We don't know if this killed them or if they just didn't like the smell, but they are gone.
—*Allene Degenhardt Percy, Illinois*

**Spread ashes** from a wood burning stove across your yard. (Use sparingly in alkaline soils, also known as "sweet" soils.) Moles will leave that area for another.
—*Paul Offutt, Lebanon, Missouri*

**I've found** that Mole-Med, a mole repellent sold through the *Gardens Alive!* catalog, works on voles as well. —*Carlen Kreutzer Stafford, Virginia*

**Plant castor beans** in your yard to discourage moles. (Castor beans are toxic. Keep children and pets away from them.) —*Janet Watson De Motte, Indiana*

**Juicy Fruit gum** never fails to eradicate moles. Carefully poke a hole into a run with your finger and insert a whole unwrapped stick of the gum. Then cover the hole, being careful not to disturb the run. We used to have *lots* of moles. Occasionally we'll find a new run, but just one or two pieces of Juicy Fruit takes care of it. —*Mary Nissley Sarcoxie, Missouri*

**We used** to cover our berries with netting to discourage birds. But it was time-consuming and a bother. So I bought some stuffed animals from a thrift store and hung them from stakes around the berries. It's comical to watch birds sail in for a bite and quickly fly away when they see the toys. —*Emmylu Lawrence Beaverton, Oregon*

**I've found** a very effective way to get rid of moles. Blend one bottle (about 4 ounces) castor oil, 10 squirts of dish detergent and a cup of water in a blender. Dilute about 1 ounce per gallon of water and pour it over the area the mole has been through. —*Carol Bozarth Poplar Bluff, Missouri*

**After gophers** destroyed all my spring bulbs, I marched into the kitchen, grabbed the hot red pepper and sprinkled it in every hole I could find. Guess what? The gophers are still around the neighborhood, but not in my yard.

Now hot red pepper is one of the most important things in my garden cart. It keeps rabbits out of my flowers and bushes, too.
—*Noreen Koehn St. Cloud, Minnesota*

> **When squirrels** started raiding my deck garden, I put out a dish of black-oil sunflower seeds and walnuts for them. Now I get the joy of watching the squirrels' antics without having them dig in my plants.
> —*Michelle Jensen*
> *Seattle, Washington*

**I use** a solar-powered security light to scare varmints away from my garden. If any movement is detected within 50 feet, the bright lights switch on. I also bait a Havahart trap with apples or peanut butter to catch any intruders that sneak past the security light. Don't use fish or meat as bait, though—I did that once and trapped a skunk.
—*Cornelius Hogenbirk*
*Waretown, New Jersey*

**Squirrels dug** up every bulb I planted until I began sprinkling just-planted areas with garlic powder. Since then, there hasn't been a bulb missing! Garlic powder keeps bugs off other flowers and plants, too.
—*Christina Phillips*
*Indianapolis, Indiana*

**I cover** deciduous tree seedlings, budding tulips and lilies with plastic onion bags from the supermarket. Light and air can get to the leaves, but hungry critters can't get through the netting to chop off the stems.
—*Eileen Weslowski*
*Pleasant Valley, New York*

**To keep rodents** from eating the bark off bushes during winter, I place a mothball at the base of each bush. This keeps rodents away from the house foundation, too. (Keep mothballs away from kids and pets.)
—*Patricia Dobbs*
*Ferryville, Wisconsin*

**Habanero peppers** will repel just about anything, including pesky squirrels. Puree a pepper in a blender with water; strain well and spray the liquid on plants. The leftover pulp can be divided among potted plants (one spoonful per pot). Also, a mixture of pepper water, cooking oil and liquid detergent will discourage insects. (Wear gloves and do not touch your eyes when using these mixes.)
—*Bettye Bunch*
*Hemphill, Texas*

**We finally found** a repellent that keeps squirrels out of our storage building. Mix 1/4 cup garlic powder, 1/4 cup sulfur powder and 2 cups cedar shavings. Then spread the mix around the inner perimeter of the building. Renew about once a year. I haven't had an invasion in 2 years.
—*Hazel Senn*
*Cowpens, South Carolina*

**To protect seedlings** we start in flats outdoors, we cover them with our old freezer basket. It's just the right size and animal-proof, too.
—*Jack and Luci Laughlin*
*Fort Wayne, Indiana*

**Squirrels and birds** were eating seeds from my plants before I had a chance to dry them. Now I hang an old bird cage in the sun and put my green seeds inside to dry. It decorates my yard, too.     —*Ruth Beck*
*North Hollywood, California*

**A squirrel was determined** to make a nest in our bedroom wall, so we put an ultrasonic device next to the wall. The squirrel left almost immediately. Then we began using it to get rid of other pests. It's harmless, noiseless to humans and inexpensive.        —*Sanford Deck*
*Chattanooga, Tennessee*

**A friend advised** brushing ripening tomatoes with garlic oil to keep squirrels away. I did, and bingo! The squirrels kept their distance, and I didn't lose any more tomatoes.
—*Marion Henry*
*Romeoville, Illinois*

**We have a lot of squirrels**, which add up to a lot of holes and uprooted plants. A horticulturist friend suggested dusting the beds with dried blood powder. The squirrels hate it, and the flowers love it— what a wonderful combination. I also use it in pots and baskets where the squirrels like to dig.
—*Wilma Clark, Columbus, Ohio*

**To keep squirrels** out of my flowers, I put silver or gold foil in a clear plastic jar, screw the lid on and set it in the garden. The sun's reflections keep the squirrels away. Red reflector lights work, too.
—*G. Kriculi, Chicago, Illinois*

**Here is** a simple way to keep squirrels from digging up and eating newly-planted bulbs. I cover the whole area with green netting, the kind that keeps birds from eating your berries. For some reason, the squirrels will not step on the netting.
—*Rose Whipple, Oneida, New York*

**Having problems** with squirrels or rabbits? Make friends with your beautician or barber! If you sprinkle hair clippings in your garden, pests won't go near it. It's free, safe for the environment and even lasts through rains. If it's windy, wet down the clippings for the first couple of days.
—*Rosemary Lake*
*Effingham, Illinois*

**Brush mineral oil** and red pepper on corn ears to prevent squirrel and raccoon damage.

—*Irene Girard*
*Claremont, New Hampshire*

**To repel skunks** that feel "at home" around your house, scatter dog hair around the entire foundation of your home.

—*Joellen Batten-Siebers*
*Moose Lake, Minnesota*

**About 30** of our newly-planted trees were eaten by elk during the evening hours. So we started a new orchard and put a motion sensor light in the center. We haven't had any problems since.

—*Kristine Jackson*
*Young, Arizona*

**We keep critters** out of our corn by surrounding the patch with squash and pumpkin vines. If we plant only one side, or one end, the raccoons enter the patch from the "open" area and keep eating until they reach the vines.

—*Elizabeth Mohs*
*Northome, Minnesota*

**I spray** a homemade solution on petunias, rosebushes and other plants to keep critters off them. Here's my recipe. Crumble five or six cheap cigars in a 2- or 3-gallon bucket, then fill it almost to the top with water. Wait several days for the water to darken, then spray the solution on plants every other week. (Leftover tobacco tea is toxic and should be kept away from children

**When toads** started burrowing in my pots and digging up the plants, I added decorative stones—the same type used to keep house cats out of indoor plants. It's worked well and also cuts down on squirrel damage.

—*Valerie Evanson*
*Phoenixville, Pennsylvania*

and pets.) It's excellent for repelling tomato and potato bugs.

—*Barbara Eddy*
*Rio Rancho, New Mexico*

**Before placing** a set gopher trap in a tunnel, spray it with perfume, and you'll catch the gopher. We heard this tip on a radio garden show and couldn't believe it would work—but it did!

—*Wanda Cartwright*
*Vista, California*

**Hide a mothball** at the base of each bush to keep rodents from eating its bark in winter. This also keeps them from flowers and the foundation of your house. (Keep mothballs away from kids and pets.)

—*Patricia Dobbs*
*Ferryville, Wisconsin*

**I fought gophers** for *over 40 years*. As a last resort, I planted five gopher purge plants in my garden and one in a neighbor's plot, two gardens away. We haven't had a gopher bother us in 5 years. These plants don't kill gophers, they just keep the pests away. (Be aware these plants can become a weed problem in many gardens.)
—*Lora Phillips*
*Sun City, California*

**Voles** were digging up my lawn, tunneling in the garden and eating my seeds and bulbs.

After trying several remedies, I decided to use a product that helps control rodents. I used a wooden spoon handle to punch holes about 15 inches apart in new mole runs and put poison labeled for voles in each hole. Within a week, I had no new runs, and the voles apparently were gone. —*Jeanette Dalton*
*Mountain Grove, Missouri*

**Moles and gophers** were digging in my raised flower beds until I planted a couple of castor beans. (Castor bean seeds are toxic, so keep away from kids and pets.) I've had no trouble since. The critters can't stand the smell. —*Ruth Twiss*
*Wray, Colorado*

**To get rid of gophers**, roll up a piece of Juicy Fruit gum, poke a small opening in the gopher's hole and drop in the gum. Be sure to use gloves so the gum doesn't pick up your scent.
—*George and Sarah Baker*
*Winnsboro, Texas*

**One whiff of pepper** was all it took to teach my dogs to stay out of my flower beds. I've sprinkled both red and black pepper throughout the beds with good results. And I don't have to worry about exposing small children to chemicals.
—*Martha Rice*
*Yakima, Washington*

**To discourage** voles (also known as meadow mice) from my plants or from eating germinating seeds, I'll toss a clove or two of garlic next to the plant or seeds.
—*Mary Isaacsen-Bright*
*Los Osos, California*

**Neighborhood dogs** were using our 1.5-acre backyard as their toilet. I cleaned up the mess, then set out several glass jars filled with clean water. It worked! The water apparently signals that the area is now for eating. I did this for 2 to 3 months, and as long as the water was clean, the dogs left no messes there.
—*Gayle Scramstad*
*Langley, British Columbia*

# CHAPTER TWELVE

# 'STOP BUGGING ME!'

THEY MAY BE SMALL, but insects are a big problem in some gardens.

So these readers have taken the pests on with home remedies that have saved their prized plants.

Remember, not all of these methods will be effective in every garden or even every year. The best way to monitor their success is to watch the results closely throughout the growing season.

We also suggest testing some of these methods (such as homemade sprays) on a few leaves first and then waiting a few days to see how your plants react.

**I like to keep** a bar of soap in my watering can. When I water my plants, they get a dose of anti-bug soap in the process. —*Susie Fisher Lewistown, Pennsylvania*

**Put a few** "feeder" goldfish in your rain barrel to keep mosquitoes and algae from becoming a problem. I put five goldfish in a 50-gallon barrel. The kids love to feed them. We move the fish to an aquarium in winter. The "fishy" rain water is great for watering plants, too. —*Becky Olson Arden Hills, Minnesota*

**I've achieved** good insect control by planting garlic and marigolds in every garden row. I alternate the two, planting one or the other every 3 feet or so. —*Yoli Quevedo Anacortes, Washington*

**Make your plants aphid-proof** with this safe and effective spray. In a blender, combine one garlic bulb, one small onion, 1 tablespoon cayenne pepper and 1 quart water. Then let the mixture steep. Add 1 tablespoon dish-washing liquid to help the other ingredients stick to the plants.

The mixture can be stored in the refrigerator for up to a week. (Wear gloves and do not to touch your eyes when using cayenne pepper.) —*Karen Ann Bland, Gove, Kansas*

**Nothing stops cutworms** better than this simple collar. Remove the bottom from a Styrofoam cup, slit one side and place around the plant, with cut sides overlapping. Push the cup into the soil to keep it from blowing over. —*Weldon Burge Newark, Delaware*

**We place wood ashes** from our fireplace around the base of fruit trees to keep bugs away. (Use sparingly in alkaline soils, also known as "sweet" soils.) —*Monica Bengston Independence, Iowa*

**Plant two or three** dill seeds in each squash hill, and you won't have any squash bugs. —*Dee Hancock, Fremont, Nebraska*

**Crop rotation** is one of the best weapons against garden pests. —*Marjorie Carey, Freeport, Florida*

**To keep box elder bugs** away from the warm side of your house in spring and fall, mix liquid dishwashing soap and water in a spray bottle. Spray the side and base of the house, repeating if necessary. —*Monica Bengston Independence, Iowa*

**Every spring**, I hang jugs of this special mix in my apple trees to keep worms away. Combine 1 cup each of water, vinegar and sugar. The recipe can be doubled or tripled. If the jug fills with insects, empty and replace with a fresh batch of the mix. —*Julie Hight Garretson, South Dakota*

**To repel** most winged insects while gardening, use Avon Skin So Soft SPF 15 Sunblock Plus, original scent. It protects you from the sun and bugs at the same time. It really works! —*Janet Cholin*
*South Williamsport, Pennsylvania*

**Put a short length** of hose in your garden to control earwigs. They will crawl inside, and you can drop the hose into a shallow bucket of water to rinse them out and then destroy them. —*Judie Wilkinson*
*Escondido, California*

**In the South**, we have wasps called dirt daubers or mud daubers. They keep the spider population in check, but their mud nests are unsightly and can ruin farm equipment. To keep them out of my dairy barn, I installed ceiling fans in each room. The fans are controlled by timers to run from daylight to dusk. This helps keep these insects from building nests. —*Ernest Vogt*
*Yantis, Texas*

**I keep** destructive insects out of my garden by relying on backyard birds. In spring, I turn in all my leaves with a spade and wait for the robins, sparrows, blackbirds and wrens to arrive to feast on the insects.

—*Mae Warrick*
*Jennings, Kansas*

**June bug grubs** damage our lawn. To prevent the bugs from laying eggs (that will hatch into new grubs), here's how we capture them.

*Grandma's Green Thumb*

**My grandma** told me to plant a row of sage in the garden to keep pests out. —*Mary Quinn Gratiot, Wisconsin*

We place a large open container, like a washtub, in the area where we have the problem. We fill it about 3/4 full of water and suspend a 60- or 100-watt light bulb a foot above it. When evening rolls around, we switch on the light. The June bugs are attracted to the light, fall into the water and drown. In the morning, we dispose of a tub full of bugs.
—*Harry Atkins, Fonthill, Ontario*

**Sprinkle powdered** garlic on your greens patch to keep insects away. I find the garlic treatment works especially well on turnip greens, mustard greens and collards. The garlic isn't harmful to the birds and does not affect the taste of the greens. —*Faye Croft Edmunds*
*Hopkinsville, Kentucky*

**Geranium-leaf** tea will keep bugs away. Pick a half-dozen leaves, steep in hot water and strain. Spray the brew on plants with a mister. For best results, repeat after every rain. It's effective, completely organic and harmless to children and pets.
—*Barbara Dege*
*Hackensack, New Jersey*

**Place 1 teaspoon** of sugar and 1 teaspoon of powdered boric acid in a covered jar. Make holes in the top large enough for ants to enter. They take the mixture back to their nest. Soon, you won't have an ant problem.
—*Helen Costello*
*Chicopee, Massachusetts*

**To prevent cutworm** damage, cut a drinking straw about 3 inches long, then slice it lengthwise. Open the straw and put it around the plant stem, then slide it into the dirt. This makes it impossible for the cutworm to get to the stem.
—*Joellen Batten-Siebers*
*Moose Lake, Minnesota*

**Bantam hens** are better at controlling insects than pesticides. They're busy all day looking for moths, snails, earwigs, etc., and they don't dig big holes in your garden like larger chickens. My apples, apricots and tomatoes seldom need anything else. —*Mrs. M. Teigen*
*Los Altos, California*

**The root maggot** seems to be our worst enemy. When I set out transplants, I surround the stems with collars made from recycled cans or containers (about 1 to 2 inches high and 4 inches in diameter). Then I fill the collars with finely crushed eggshells, which prevents the fly from laying eggs next to the plant stem. Since I began using this method, I haven't lost a single plant.
—*Mrs. David Sharkey*
*Creswell, Oregon*

**To protect** garden plants from slugs, spread a layer of crushed eggshells around them. —*Marie Blahut*
*Yorkton, Saskatchewan*

**Spread cornmeal** about an inch thick around tree trunks or plant stems where ants are a problem. After watering or a rainfall, fluff up the meal with your fingers and replace as needed. —*Toye Spence*
*Baker City, Oregon*

**Instead of spraying** for whiteflies, we paint sticks of wood yellow, then smear them with petroleum jelly. The flies are attracted by the yellow color and get stuck in the jelly. —*Elizabeth Srutowski*
*Mesa, Arizona*

**When slugs and snails** shredded my hostas, I asked several area beauty shops to save hair clippings for me. The following spring, I put a ring of hair around each hosta. This year they're beautiful.
—*Carol Bozarth*
*Poplar Bluff, Missouri*

**Plant dill** with all your vine crops. This versatile herb does extra duty in repelling squash bugs and cucumber beetles.—*Karen Ann Bland*
*Gove, Kansas*

**To keep** flies away, plant savory in pots next to your house. Flies don't like the smell. Living on a farm with livestock close by, we've tried this many times, and it works.
—*Roxann Bistline, Brandon, Iowa*

**I save plastic** milk bottles, cut holes in the sides and put a tablespoon of slug bait in each one. The slugs will find it, the bait stays dry, and other critters can't get to it. (Keep slug bait from kids and pets.)
—*Dorothy Simons*
*Bremerton, Washington*

**Bothered by hornets**, wasps and bees? I'm allergic to their stings, so hanging moth cakes on our deck has been a lifesaver. We also put them under the eaves—anywhere there might be nests. They don't like the smell and fly far away to build their nests.
—*Margaret Lindow*
*Suamico, Wisconsin*

**To reduce** the bug population, we make our yard inviting to the birds that eat lots of insects. We planted mountain ash, honeysuckle, crab apples and a Juneberry tree. We also have a bird feeder and two birdbaths next to the garden. —*Azalea Wright*
*Forest Lake, Minnesota*

**I sprinkle a mixture** of garlic powder and flour on plants to repel bugs, especially cabbage flies. Use sparingly, as it will get pasty on the leaves if applied too thickly.
—*Elaine Doyle*
*Onalaska, Wisconsin*

**To trap slugs**, mix brewer's yeast and water in a small cat-food can and place it in the garden. I've also discovered a successful way to wipe out ants—pour white vinegar on their hills and their paths into the house.
—*Madelyn Kinkade*
*Lake Milton, Ohio*

**To keep** yellow jackets from interrupting your gardening or other backyard activities, create a yellow jacket "jail" out of an unwashed 1-gallon plastic milk jug. Cut a small upside-down "V"-shaped flap about two-thirds of the way down one side of the jug. Pour an inch of fruit punch into the jug and screw the top on. Use rubber bands to hang the jug in your picnic area or near the garbage. The yellow jackets will be attracted to the juice, invite themselves into the jug, but won't be able to get out.
—*Patricia Reed, Huron, Ohio*

**Use a** season-extending fabric (these floating row covers are sold under names such as Reemay and Frost Blanket) over beets, spinach and Swiss chard to prevent the leaf-miner fly from laying eggs that hatch into leaf-tunneling larvae. The row covers also can be used to prevent root-maggot damage in radishes.

—*Joyce Cooksey*
*Braintree, Massachusetts*

**Invite toads** into your garden—each will consume about 3,000 garden pests a month! I make my garden inviting to toads by not using toxic pesticides. I also place clay pots with a piece missing from around the rim upside-down on the soil. This provides cool shady areas. (Toads rest in the shade during the day and forage at night.) If you mulch, the toads will find plenty of hiding places on their own.

—*Weldon Burge, Newark, Delaware*

**To keep ants** out of the house, sprinkle a solid line of kitchen cleanser along the door sill. One application at our patio entrance and front door lasted at least 3 years. Low-cost generic products work great because they are more grainy than name brands. —*Alice Goslow*
*Clinton Township, Michigan*

**To check** for cutworms, dig gently around a plant stem with your fingers. The caterpillars are easy to recognize—when disturbed, they curl into a "C", for cutworm!

—*Sharon Scholz, Oakland, Oregon*

**Cover cabbage** heads with nylons to keep out the white moth or butterfly that produces green worms.

—*Ellen Gaugler*
*Hoselaw, Alberta*

**Grab the salt** shaker when you see white moths or butterflies around cabbage or broccoli. Sprinkle salt on each cabbage head and broccoli plant while damp and repeat after it rains. Last year, I froze over 30 bunches of broccoli and found only one worm in them.

—*Dee Hancock, Fremont, Nebraska*

**For slugs**, fill shallow plates or small cans with honey or yeast and place in the soil, with the opening at ground level. The slugs will crawl in and die. —*Mary Stager*
*Silver Bay, Minnesota*

**Here's my tip** for getting rid of Japanese beetles. Cut the top off a gallon milk jug, fill it halfway with water, then add a drop of dish detergent. When you see beetles, hold the jug right under the infested plant and give it a quick tap. The beetles drop into the water. The detergent coats their wings so they can't fly back out. It's easy, cheap and not harmful to other critters.

—*Carole Smithers, Columbus, Ohio*

**My brother-in-law** taught me to sprinkle sulfur in potato rows. You won't have any bugs, and the sulfur won't affect the taste of the potatoes.

—*Ellen Sanders, Iuka, Mississippi*

**This is the cheapest** easiest solution I've found to kill bugs. Put a pinch of chewing tobacco in an old nylon stocking and drop in boiling water until the water turns dark brown. (Tobacco tea is toxic and should be kept away from children and pets.) In a 20-gallon sprayer that attaches to a garden hose, mix 1 cup of the juice with 1 cup baby shampoo or liquid dish soap. I spray this on my garden the first evening of each month in the growing season, and everything looks greenhouse-grown. —*Nancy Hardin*
*Stanwood, Michigan*

**Here's a cheap** natural way to repel aphids and spider mites. Mix 1/3 cup cooking oil and 1 teaspoon baking soda in a jar; keep covered until needed. Combine 2 teaspoons of mixture with 1 cup water in a sprayer. —*Henryette Marshall*
*Jensen Beach, Florida*

**For the past** 2 years, I've planted garlic cloves 2 to 3 feet apart in each row of potatoes, and I haven't had *any* potato bugs. —*Ruby Saccone*
*Clarksburg, West Virginia*

**To prevent** scabs on potatoes, sprinkle pine needles over the bottom of the potato trench before planting.
—*Mary Jones*
*Chaska, Minnesota*

**Cut garlic cloves** into small pieces and place some in each hill with corn seed to keep worms from eating the mature ears of corn.
—*Julia Fletcher, Medford, Oregon*

**Put "popped" popcorn** in your bird feeder to attract insect-eating birds. I have blue jays, grackles, flickers, woodpeckers and one mixed-up robin at my feeders every morning. After a breakfast of popcorn and seed, they spend the whole day in my garden, eating bugs. Be sure the corn is popped in grease or oil—that attracts the birds.
—*Kathleen Bollinger*
*Tarentum, Pennsylvania*

**To kill** Colorado potato bugs, spray plants with Epsom salts and then sprinkle with dry wheat bran. Reapply after each rain. We'd tried everything, and this method gave us the best potato crop we'd had in years.
—*Albert Buening*
*Effingham, Illinois*

**When you pull onions,** cut off the tops and toss them over cabbages and other plants in the cabbage family to discourage green worms. —*Virginia Bohm*
*Princeton, Illinois*

**To control** bean beetles, dust plants with flour.
—*Shasta Marshall, Winfield, Iowa*

**When Sevin** insecticide failed to control Colorado potato bugs in my garden, the Farmers Co-op told me to dust with Rotenone powder.

Within 24 hours, the bugs were gone, and they never returned—even though nearby gardens were thoroughly infested. Using Rotenone on my neighbors' badly damaged plots produced the same results. —*H.S. Cowan Jr.*
*Linthicum Heights, Maryland*

---

**Keep grasshoppers** off cantaloupes by slipping the fruit into a pantyhose leg. Don't make it too tight on the stem end and be sure any runs in the hose are next to the ground, or the grasshoppers will eat through them. I've used this on other produce, too. —*Joellen Aichele*
*Steele, North Dakota*

---

**When planting** cucumber, squash or pumpkin seeds, sprinkle some Sevin in the hole, and beetles will leave the plants alone. I lost seedlings to bugs for years until a neighbor passed on this tip.

—*Dorothy Mixa*
*Naperville, Illinois*

**I use plastic** margarine tubs to help keep slugs from my tomatoes and hostas. I cut several 1/2-inch holes around the top of the tub just below the rim. (Several overlapping holes made with a paper punch will do the trick.) Fill the tub up to the bottom of the holes with beer. Place the lid on top to help keep out rain and put it near the plants you want to protect. I dig a 1-1/2-inch-deep hole to sink the tub so it doesn't tip.
—*Alice Dunsdon*
*Glenwood, Iowa*

**Here's a recipe** for organic pest control. Mix cayenne pepper with 2 teaspoons soapy water, 1 cup salad oil and manure. Dilute to half-strength with water, pour around plants and then apply dry wood ashes. —*Yoli Quevedo*
*Anacortes, Washington*

**When planting vegetables**, I wrap a small piece of newspaper around the stem above and below the soil. This prevents cutworms from getting to the plants.
—*Norma Wolff*
*Cranberry Township, Pennsylvania*

**To get rid of ants** in the garden and house, mix 4 teaspoons powdered boric acid, 1 cup sugar and 3 cups water. Bring to a boil; cool and pour some into a small bottle. Puncture holes in the lid. Stick a straw in one hole and put the other end of the straw where you've seen ants. Refill the bottles as needed. Ants will be gone within 2 weeks. Store in a cool place and be sure to label the bottle "ant poison". Keep away from children.

—*Grace Paulson*
*Castro Valley, California*

**I mix** equal amounts of vinegar and water and spray it on slugs. They dissolve instantly.

—*Mildred Britton*
*Glendale, California*

**My mother** suggested this successful, natural and inexpensive solution for controlling slugs. Save all your eggshells, bake them for about 10 minutes, then crush and store them until ready to use. In spring, place a wide band of shells around the base of your plants. The baked shells are so sharp the slugs can't cross them. It works.

—*Barbara Cormach*
*Red Deer, Alberta*

**My family** has used this tip for cutworms for three generations. Cut strips of brown paper (grocery bags work great) a couple of inches wide and 3 to 4 inches long. As you plant your tomatoes, wrap the strips around the stem. About 1 to 2 inches of the paper should be visible above the soil.
—*Marilyn Fils, Creston, Iowa*

**To protect plants** from cutworms, sprinkle a ring of cornmeal around each one. —*Wanda Burrer Wing, North Dakota*

**To keep** Japanese beetles from chewing bush beans, plant tall marigolds (ones that stand at least 3 feet) at the ends of each row. The beetles love the marigold blossoms and will stay off the beans. Keep in mind that, for this to work, the marigolds must be taller than the beans. —*Mrs. Russell Neiswander Sugarcreek, Ohio*

**To catch flies**, mix 2 cups water, 1/2 cup sugar and 1/2 cup white vinegar and pour into a fruit jar. Punch holes in the lid large enough for the flies to get through. Put it outside the door, and you'll catch flies before they get into your house.
—*Sharon Herren*
*Kearney, Nebraska*

**I always plant radishes** with my cucumbers and let most of them go to seed. I don't know why, but I have little or no trouble with beetles when the radishes are blooming.
—*Betty Nelson, Des Moines, Iowa*

**Here's a simple** inexpensive solution for cutworms. Stick toothpicks into the ground right next to young seedlings. This prevents worms from cutting through the stem. And because toothpicks are biodegradable, there's nothing to clean up later. —*Roberta Kelly South China, Maine*

## Grandma's Green Thumb

**Grandma** kept worms out of her corn by filling an old dish-soap bottle with vegetable oil and squirting it onto the silks. She did this about once a week and after it rained, until the corn was ready to harvest.
—Jayme Litaker, Searcy, Arkansas

**As soon** as silk appears on sweet corn, sprinkle black pepper on the end of each ear. Repeat once or twice until the corn is ready. No more worms! I also sprinkle pepper on the seed heads of onions to keep out tiny spiders that eat the seeds.
—Mrs. Glen Lambright
Topeka, Indiana

**To protect** fruit from insects, hang small cans of sugar-water from the branches. The bugs and insects will be drawn to the cans instead of the fruit.
—Janet Watson
De Motte, Indiana

**Turn a roofing shingle** into an effective, inexpensive and chemical-free slug trap. Cut the shingle into three pieces and lay them rough sides up in the garden. Check the shingles during the hottest time of day. Slugs will cling to the undersides and can be destroyed.
—Audrey De Simone
Montgomery City, Missouri

**To trap slugs** and snails, we put beer in small cat-food cans and set them in the ground so the top is level with the soil. It's also a safe way to control these pests without endangering birds and other animals.
—Orman Woodward
West Linn, Oregon

**Slugs** were devouring my strawberries until I dusted the ground well with diatomaceous earth, which is available at garden centers. No more slugs. I reapply after each rain.
—Darlene Harper
Arkansas City, Kansas

**To keep ants** from following a trail into your house, garage or shed, wipe the trail area with vinegar. It destroys the scent, which the ants follow.
—Melinda Myers
Milwaukee, Wisconsin

**Dawn brand** of dish washing soap or Murphy's Oil Soap can stop pests from destroying your flowers. Put a little of either into an empty spray bottle, fill with water, mix and spray your blooms.
—Peggy Goff
Mansfield, Pennsylvania

**To prevent** slug damage to tomatoes, circle plants with a layer of cornmeal about 1/8 inch thick and about 3 inches away from the plant's stem.
—Gloria Tjernlund
Ironwood, Michigan

127

**Lemons** will discourage ants from entering your home. Just put lemon slices around your doorway or wherever ants are getting in. Within 2 hours, they should be gone.

—*Kathyrn Gemmill*
*York Springs, Pennsylvania*

**To get rid** of slugs, I place hollowed-out orange rinds upside-down in my garden. The next morning I'll collect the rinds. They're usually full of slugs and snails. It's a quick, easy and safe solution. —*Marion Taylor*
*Calgary, Alberta*

**I sprinkle wood ashes** on my cabbage patch to drive the bugs away. (Use sparingly in alkaline soils, also known as "sweet" soils.)
—*Anna Fay Swapp*
*Silver City, New Mexico*

**If you have trouble** with cutworms, wrap a 1/2-inch-wide strip of aluminum foil around young plant stems at ground level. The foil will expand as the plants grow.
—*Ruth Walker*
*Meyersdale, Pennsylvania*

**Mosquitoes** chew me up whenever I work in the garden. So I mix 1 tablespoon of Murphy's Oil Soap with a gallon of water. Then I put it in a spray bottle and spritz between the rows where I want to work. This mixture also can be sprayed around bushes, picnic tables, swings and seating areas. It really drives the mosquitoes away. —*Marie Baker*
*Decatur, Indiana*

**A friend** in Nebraska gave me this recipe to protect apple trees from the gray fruit fly. Put one banana peel, 1 cup sugar, 1 cup white vinegar and 1/2 gallon water in a gallon jug. Shake well, open and place on a sturdy low branch. This method has worked for years.

If you drive through this area, you'll see many apple trees with milk jugs wedged in the bottom branches. —*Rosemary Dougherty*
*Lenox, Iowa*

**If you see** even *one* potato bug, mulch your garden with straw spread 6 inches deep. The confused bugs can't find the plants and just crawl around in the straw. Works every time.

—*Mary Ann Lengacher*
*Grabill, Indiana*

**Diatomaceous earth** will kill all kinds of crawling insects (slugs, cockroaches, ants, beetles, silverfish, crickets, millipedes and earwigs) both indoors and out. It's odorless and non-staining. I've found it works well in cracks and crevices, behind stoves and sinks, in garbage cans, window frames, attics and basements.

—*Mary Davis, Billings, Missouri*

**I use empty** beverage bottles to make effective traps for yellow jackets, wasps and biting flies. Just fill the bottles half full with sugar-water. Winged pests have no trouble finding the small bottle opening, but they can't find their way back out.
—*Cornelius Hogenbirk*
*Waretown, New Jersey*

**To keep cutworms** from destroying my cabbages and tomatoes, I place a large nail right beside each plant when I set them out. The nail prevents the cutworm from wrapping itself around the plant to eat it.
—*Mary Hiter, Benton, Kentucky*

**Living near** the Pacific Ocean, we have summer year-round and the bugs that go with it. Mothballs are one of the best deterrents. Just place them in the ground 3 to 5 feet apart.

Your uninvited visitors leave, whether they're creeping, crawling or flying. (Keep mothballs away from kids and pets.)
—*Charleene Tuck*
*San Diego, California*

**This recipe** keeps pests off my flowers. Mix 1 cup Epsom salts, 1/4 cup Ivory liquid, 2 tablespoons liquid fertilizer and 5 gallons of water. I put it in a watering can and sprinkle it on.    —*Evelyn Quigley*
*Bally, Pennsylvania*

**I fill** little plastic margarine containers with beer and place them within my raspberry bushes. It helps keep black beetles (also known as "picnic beetles") away. They'll go to the beer and will leave your berries alone.    —*Minnie Nunemaker*
*St. Johns, Missouri*

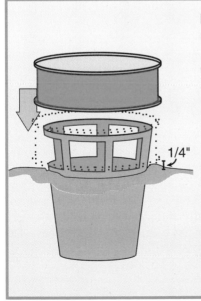

**I didn't believe** beer would kill slugs…but it really works. Place a 5-1/2-ounce pet-food can upside down on the top of an 8-ounce yogurt cup. Draw a line along the bottom of the can onto the yogurt cup, then cut four 1-1/2 x 1-inch square holes in it 1/8 inch above the line.

Bury the cup in soil so the line sits about 1/4 inch above the ground. Fill the bottom of the cup with beer and place the can on top (upside-down).

The can used as a "lid" helps the beer last longer. It only needs to be replaced every 5 to 7 days. This trap catches sow bugs, too.    —*Pat Auer*
*Fort Walton Beach, Florida*

**To keep away** pesky garden insects, make a strong tea from water and coarse chewing tobacco. Spray it on flowers and vegetables. It works! (Leftover tobacco tea is toxic and should be kept away from children and pets.)
—*Bettye Anderson*
*Fredericksburg, Texas*

**To eliminate** blight and bugs, mulch your entire garden with grass clippings once your plants have sprouted. (Do not use clippings from invasive grasses or lawns recently treated with weed killers.) This also holds moisture and fertilizes your plants.
—*Mrs. Herbert Luchsinger Jr.*
*Columbus, Nebraska*

**A senior citizen** gave me this aphid-control recipe. Mix water, organic liquid soap, ground cayenne pepper and any kind of fertilizer. Spray on infested plants, covering all surfaces including the bottoms of the leaves. Your problems will be over. (Wear gloves and do not to touch your eyes when using cayenne pepper.)
—*Yoli Quevedo*
*Anacortes, Washington*

**Use hedge balls** (also called hedge apples or osage oranges) to keep spiders, bugs and mice out of your house. They are available in the produce section of some grocery stores and at garden centers.

Put several of the green softball-sized fruits in the basement or lower level of your home to keep it free of pests. Be sure to place them on a piece of foil or other leakproof material. As they deteriorate, they may secrete a material that can damage floors. After a year, they will dry into brown balls, but they will still repel insects.
—*Susan Gebauer*
*Mountain Lake, Minnesota*

**Here's the best way** I've found to dust fungicide and insecticide on roses, dahlias and other flowers. Drop a cup full of fungicide or insecticide powder into one leg of an old pair of pantyhose. It will drop right to the foot and then you can shake a nice fine dusting onto your flowers. Spreading it this way eliminates clumping. (Carefully read all fungicide and insecticide labels. Wear protective clothing or gloves as directed.)
—*Mary Oberlin*
*Selins Grove, Pennsylvania*

**Here's a solution** I make to keep whiteflies and aphids away from my plants. Mix 1 teaspoon of dishwashing detergent and 3 tablespoons of Tabasco sauce. Put it into a spray bottle and spray it on roses, flowers and the branches of fruit trees. (Do not spray the fruit; this solution will give it a hot flavor.)
—*Judie Wilkinson*
*Escondido, California*

# CHAPTER THIRTEEN

# PUTTING YOUR GARDEN TO BED

AFTER THE GROWING SEASON is over, you don't have to stop gardening. Some of our backyard "experts" (the readers who contributed tips to this book) suggest that their gardens thrive because of the extra attention they give them at the end of the season.

Try a few of these tips to tuck in your garden for a winter's rest. You may be surprised how refreshed it is when it awakens next growing season.

**Every fall**, I put my garden to bed by raking all my leaves into it.
—*Ann Proffit, Bellbrook, Ohio*

**To save geraniums** through winter, gently dig out the plants before a killing frost. Shake off the soil and place them in brown paper bags. After a couple of days, pull another brown bag over the top and store the plants in a cold cellar (with temperatures in the 40s). In early spring, remove them from the bags, clean off the dead leaves, pot them in soil and water well. Prune to desired height. Some of my geraniums have overwintered this way for more than 20 years. —*Mrs. Harold Beisel Moorefield, Ontario*

**My dad covers** his entire garden with old carpeting in the fall. In winter, he can split wood there without getting muddy. —*Barb Wagner Willmar, Minnesota*

**After raking** autumn leaves into bags, I pile the bags in an out-of-the-way corner. In spring, I line the aisles of the garden with old newspapers, then cover them with the bagged leaves. The combination of newspaper and leaves holds in moisture and minimizes weeds. It also provides a nice place to walk when the rest of the garden is muddy. In fall, all this is turned under for organic matter, and the cycle continues. —*Nita Young Nebo, North Carolina*

**I plant** dahlias, gladiolus and cannas in black plastic greenhouse pots, then set the potted plants into the soil. In fall, I just lift the pots and store them for the winter. This saves time and money. And it prevents me from injuring tubers and corms with a shovel. —*Charlene Margetiak Norwalk, Ohio*

**I put my garden** to bed by raking the fallen leaves to form a blanket over the top, then I till the leaves into the soil.

This aerates the soil, and the leaves have broken down by spring to provide nutrients for more plant growth. —*Samuel Mott St. Michaels, Maryland*

**To protect perennials** from harsh winters, cover beds with landscape cloth. This allows moisture and air to go through while still protecting the plants. Since it blocks light, remove it as soon as plants start growing in spring. Cleanup is easy. Even my tea roses do well under this covering.
—*Roberta Card-Clark Superior, Wisconsin*

**If you don't** want to dig up dahlia tubers each fall, try my method. After the first frost, I cut down the dahlia stalks, place three layers of cardboard over the bed of tubers and cover it with 3 to 4 inches of soil to hold the cardboard in place. Then I top that with 6 to 8 inches of leaves.

After all danger of frost has passed in spring, I remove the leaves, soil and cardboard. If the tips

of the plants are already peeking through the soil, I cover them with leaves or soil to protect them. With this method, I seldom lose any plants. (Gardeners in more northerly areas should play it safe and bring tubers inside during winter months.)
—*Ethel Gepford*
*Miamisburg, Ohio*

**I spread and till** compost and manure on my garden, then cover the surface with newspapers and straw. In spring, there are no weeds to pull, and the garden is immediately ready to plant. (This method works in areas with mild winters.)
—*Dorothy Simons*
*Bremerton, Washington*

**When frost** is on the way, pull up tomato plants with the fruits still on. Hang the plants upside-down over the garage rafters. The tomatoes will continue to ripen for quite some time.
—*Jan Sherman*
*Springfield, Missouri*

**Each fall**, I till several loads of manure and all our leaves and clippings into the garden. It doesn't seem to matter whether the manure is fresh or composted. We get the same good results either way.
—*David Halbrook*
*Kings Beach, California*

**In areas with mild winters**, try this fall routine for a weed-free garden next spring. Pull the spent vegetation from your beds, work in compost you've been saving since spring and mulch with a heavy cov-

---

### Tip from Our "Landlady"

*In fall, cut healthy pest-free annual flowers with a mulching mower and then till everything into the soil. Your soil will be rich and ready for planting in the spring.* —*Gail Russell*
*Reiman Publications*

---

ering of marsh hay or straw. In spring, just pull back the hay and plant your garden. —*Ruth Weaver*
*Joshua, Texas*

**Every summer**, I take photos of my gardens. In fall, I mount them in a lined notebook and write comments under each photo. I record what I planted that year, plants I'd like to try and tips to improve next year's gardens.

It's a big help to write these things down when they're fresh in my mind. Then when spring rolls around, I'm ready to go.
—*Karen Andrews*
*Petersburg, Ontario*

**In autumn**, put a good layer of fallen leaves in your raspberry patch. The leaves settle during winter and protect the tender roots. In spring, they break down into a good soil additive when the plants begin to grow. I've had large wonderful berries for quite a number of years.
—*Carol Ramsey*
*Rochester Hills, Michigan*

**133**

**To harvest seeds** of flowers like cockscomb (*celosia*), I put the flowers in a brown paper bag to dry. The seeds soon fall off and can easily be saved.
*—Monica Bengston*
*Independence, Iowa*

**The clay** in our garden soil tends to become packed. Adding maple leaves in fall helps keep it looser and moist. *—Mary Mahn*
*Ravenna, Illinois*

**In fall**, don't pull out the dead annuals in your garden. They'll come out much easier in spring after the roots have rotted. If you cover your beds with leaves in fall, the annuals also help hold the leaves in place.
*—Jodie Stevenson*
*Export, Pennsylvania*

**Putting my garden** to bed for the winter is a process that actually starts in midsummer. When annuals fade, I remove them and mulch the beds for winter. By late October, I've emptied the pots on my patio and cut back the few remaining perennials. When you make cleanup an ongoing process, it isn't so overwhelming. *—Marcia Briggs*
*Pittsburgh, Pennsylvania*

**When I dig up dahlias,** I save one blossom from each plant and keep it with its tuberous root. I hose down the tubers and dry them in the sun. Clean dry tubers and accompanying flowers are labeled and stored in the coolest part of the basement. This method helps me remember the color and flower type the next spring. *—Azalea Wright*
*Forest Lake, Minnesota*

**At the end** of the season, I disinfect all my tools and tomato cages with a solution of 1 part bleach to 9 parts water. This also can be used during the growing season when handling diseased plants.
*—Sue Gronholz*
*Columbus, Wisconsin*

**I put all my autumn leaves** in the chicken house and let the hens and rooster work them over during winter. In spring, I put the leaves on the garden. By then they're easy to work into the soil with the tiller.
*—Leo Bexten*
*Ottawa Lake, Michigan*

**After raking leaves** in fall, I run the lawn mower over them to chop them up before I bag them. Then I add 2 cups of 8-8-8 fertilizer to each bag, close with a twist-tie and neatly stack them in a pile in the garden. Because our winters are mild, I have instant compost come spring.
*—Sue Crumpton*
*Pleasant Grove, Alabama*

**Some self-sowing seeds** are ground cherry and cherry tomato. When we cultivate our garden, we spare a few of these plants because they reward us with a bit of fruit here and there.

*—John and Eula Henline*
*Mitchell, South Dakota*

**Wintering geraniums** is fairly easy. Before frost hits, pull them up and place them in brown grocery bags. Store under the basement stairs with the bags open.

At potting time, trim to 4 to 6 inches, place in pots and put back under the stairs. When plants begin to grow, they're ready to set outside but may need to be protected from the cold.

*—Josephine Slemmons*
*Jackson, Michigan*

**If you plan to start** a new garden bed in fall, cover the area with old carpet in summer. By autumn, the grass will be dead, and the soil will be moist and ready to till.

*—Barb Wagner, Willmar, Minnesota*

**If you are tired** of planting dahlias in spring only to have to dig them out after the fall frost hits, try this easy method. Plant the tuberous roots in large black pots, like the ones shrubs are sold in. After frost, cut off the tops of the plants and allow the pots to dry well. Then carry the pots into the cellar to keep the roots from freezing. Next spring, carry them back outside, add more soil and water well.

*—A. Kunasek, Abingdon, Maryland*

**To keep sunflower heads** for winter feed, cover them with panty hose in fall. This will save the bulk of the seeds for the birds that stay in winter.

*—Wilbur Jensen*
*Onalaska, Wisconsin*

**In fall**, we take all the garden extras (vegetables, stalks, vines, etc.) and drag them to the compost pile. Then we till the garden well. In spring, we just add composted horse manure, and our gardens are ready to go.

*—Martha Odell*
*Sidney Center, New York*

**Save branches** from discarded Christmas trees to protect perennials, bulbs or dwarf shrubs from winter exposure.

*—Becky Gore*
*Evansville, Indiana*

**To grow stronger** tomato plants, sprinkle the bed with bone meal and a 2-foot-deep layer of straw in autumn. During winter, tuck coffee grounds, eggshells and fruit and vegetable peelings under the straw. In spring, remove the straw or till it in with the rest of the materials. The soil will be rich and crumbly.

*—Bobbie Jones, Huntington, Texas*

# CHAPTER FOURTEEN

# TOOLS OF THE TRADE

YOU HAVE TO give plenty of credit to our resource-ful readers for this chapter. They found dozens of us-es for items most people would never think of.

Many of these suggestions are great ways to recy-cle. However, be careful to thoroughly clean the items you're recycling before using them in the garden.

And be sure to clearly label the new contents of re-cycled containers...especially if they are being used for potentially toxic items.

**Mark a hoe** handle with the measurements of 12, 18 and 24 inches. This helps space plants or rows uniformly and saves time.
—*Charlotte Wiggins, Geneva, Ohio*

**Save the silica** packets you find in vitamin bottles and shoe boxes. Place one packet in a plastic bag with dry seeds you've collected from your garden. This keeps them dry and prevents deterioration, so more seeds will germinate when planted. I've kept seeds for several years this way. —*Marcy Samat Chicago, Illinois*

**To manage** a heavy sprayer, I use a pull cart meant for carrying golf clubs. The spray tank fits nicely and is easy to move through the garden. This "sprayer on wheels" also reduces my spraying time.
—*Joanne Fluharty Waynesville, Ohio*

**I always keep** a sturdy knife with a 10- to 12-inch blade in my gardening basket. When I want to share plants with a friend, it's much easier to make a clean cut without disturbing the remaining plant. The part being removed can be lifted out with a small spade, shovel or old pie server. —*Jean Reichow Ray, Minnesota*

**A child's** plastic sled works great for transporting flats of plants and other items from the car to the garden. —*Rita Christianson Glenburn, North Dakota*

**Powdered insecticide** made a mess when I applied it from the bag. Now I use a metal flour shaker—the kind with holes on top that you use when you roll out pie crust. It makes a great sprinkler and spreads the dust evenly, with less waste and mess. (Clearly label the shaker for safety.) —*Ruth Ann Luker Sellersburg, Indiana*

**I dig holes** for planting sweet corn with a child's ski pole. The long handle saves my back, and the ring (called a basket) at the end of the pole keeps the depth of the holes consistent. I drop a kernel into each hole. Then I use my foot to drag soil to cover it and pat it in place. It works great. —*Rose Gasper Elsie, Michigan*

**When my mother** threw away her mailbox, I decided to recycle it. I placed it in my garden and use it as a little garden shed. I keep twine, a shovel, clippers and extra gloves in it.
—*Tamala Bigger St. Clair, Michigan*

**When I garden**, my hands get so dry that they crack and bleed. At bedtime, I coat my hands with Bag Balm (an udder cream used on dairy cows), then put on white cotton gloves and go to sleep. In the morning, my skin is as soft as a baby's. (Petroleum jelly can be substituted for Bag Balm.) —*Donna Marek Perrinton, Michigan*

**Don't throw away** a bucket just because it has a leak in the bottom. Use it to water plants slowly. Fill the bucket with water and place it so the hole is near the plant stem. The water will seep out slowly, giving every drop a chance to soak into the ground right at the plant's roots. —*Leonard Sensenig McAlisterville, Pennsylvania*

**A pan** designed to catch oil drained from your car's engine is a great garden helper. As long as the pan has not been used for motor oil, it's perfect for soaking moss-lined hanging baskets in liquid fertilizer overnight. One with handles also makes it easy to carry plants and other items to and from the garden. —*Anne Ziebold Fremont, Ohio*

**Here's a quick method** for hulling strawberries. Push a drinking straw up through the bottom, and the stem pops out. —*Kelley Tippery Gaylord, Michigan*

**A shoe caddy** hangs in my garage to store garden tools, gloves, garden shoes and any other items that will fit in the compartments. —*Sharon Van Den Heuvel Green Bay, Wisconsin*

**An empty bleach bottle** can be used to make 24 to 28 plant markers. Cut out the label area and make one vertical cut. This will produce a long rectangle, which can be cut into strips 3/4-inch to 1-inch wide.

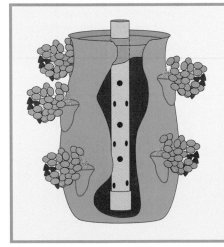

**I like planting** in strawberry jars, but it can be difficult to water the bottom plants. My husband cut a piece of PVC pipe about the depth of the pot, capped the bottom and drilled holes at different intervals up and down the pipe. When planting, place the pipe in the center while filling the jar with potting mix. Then pour water into the top of the pipe to water *all* of the plants. —*Judith Weeks, Hoxie, Kansas*

You can stick the markers right in the ground, or punch a hole in one end and attach them with twist-ties or tacks to wooden stakes.

Write plant names on the strips with a black laundry pen. The ink will last a year or more.

—*Wilbur Horning, Westlake, Ohio*

**When you plant seeds** that need to be just slightly covered with soil, it's difficult not to plant them too deep. So I use an old crank-style flour sifter to sprinkle the dirt over the seeds. —*Rachel Maendel Elka Park, New York*

**Use paint sticks** for plant markers. There is plenty of room for writing with a permanent marker.

—*Rose Whipple, Oneida, New York*

**I use a large** sharp kitchen knife to cut chives, iris, peonies, etc., in fall. It's much faster than using shears.

—*Valerie Giesbrecht*
*Othello, Washington*

**Save plastic film canisters** to store your dried flower seeds. I use a marker to identify the contents of white canisters. If the canisters are black, I label them with a piece of masking tape.

—*Mary Moore Ritchie*
*Raleigh, North Carolina*

**The wreath** support tripods used for floral and cemetery displays make ideal supports for peppers, eggplants and many tall flowers. For peppers, place the tripod over the plant when it's small and tie it to the supports with pantyhose. (Cut *across* pantyhose to make different-sized loops.)

This method also can be used to support tall heavy-stemmed flowers, like blazing star and cosmos. Tripods can be used without ties for climbers, like sweet peas, morning glories, garden peas and pole beans.

—*Diane Covington*
*Winterville, Georgia*

**For the past** 30 years, one of my favorite garden gadgets has been a tile cutter (linoleum knife) with a curved blade, available at most hardware stores. I use it to dig weeds, cut sod for a new flower bed, scrape weed and grass sprouts out of sidewalk cracks, remove sucker shoots and cut flowers to bring indoors. It's the handiest tool I've ever used. —*Sally Bashline*
*Rives Junction, Michigan*

**A 2-liter soft drink bottle** cut in half makes a great greenhouse. I put a soil-filled peat pot planted with seeds into a flowerpot set on a saucer. Then I water and cover it with the bottle top. The peat pot makes transplanting easy.

—*Carol Brown*
*Sumner, Washington*

**I use an old tin** barrel placed under a down spout to collect rainwater. Then I use it to water the plants in my hanging baskets and containers.
—*Pearl Fjugstad*
*Randle, Washington*

**A pointed** mason's trowel is perfect for setting out bedding plants in spring.
—*Rita Christianson*
*Gelburn, North Dakota*

**Keep shovels** and spades in good condition and recycle your used motor oil at the same time. Fill a 5-gallon bucket with sand. After servicing your lawn mower in spring, pour the old motor oil in the bucket of sand. Stick shovels and spades into the bucket whenever you're done with them. Next time you want them, you'll know where they are—and they'll be clean and rust-free.

All you have to do is wipe off the residue.
—*Georgia Stewart*
*Hebron, Illinois*

**For years**, I've carried a painter's "5-in-1 tool" when gardening. The blade has a curved portion to clean paint roller covers, plus a screwdriver and putty knife.

It works great for scraping caked dirt from shovels and other garden tools, and undercutting grass and weeds. It's small enough to get around plants without damaging them and strong enough to chop out really tough weed stems and roots.
—*Charles Brown*
*Melvern, Kansas*

**Save nylon hosiery** to tie up tomato plants. Their elasticity helps plants grow as large as they want.
—*Patricia Ernst, Cincinnati, Ohio*

# More Uses for Milk Jugs

**My husband**, George, uses 1-gallon plastic milk jugs to water our tomatoes. He makes a small hole in one bottom corner of the jug with an ice pick, fills it with water, caps it and places it next to the plant. The water takes a couple of hours to seep out. Not a drop is wasted because the plant has chance to absorb it all.
—*R. Mercedes Wilkinson*
*White Oak, Pennsylvania*

**To protect** tender tomato plants from frost, fill gallon milk jugs with water and surround the plants in colder areas. It will absorb enough heat during the day to keep the

**A steak knife** works better than anything I've used for digging out weeds and grass. Here's another tip. If you're filling a big flowerpot, put some foam packing "peanuts" in the bottom before adding soil. The pot won't be nearly as heavy.
—*Lorene Leebrick*
*Shelbyville, Tennessee*

**Ever try** to get a fence post out of the ground? It's not easy unless you use a pump-handle bumper jack. Wrap a heavy chain around the bottom part of the post. Hook the chain to the jack and simply lift the post out of the ground.
—*Cathie Huguenin*
*Stevensville, Montana*

**Make berry-picking easy** with a 6-pint strawberry box and a strip of lawn chair webbing long enough to go around your neck and hang at waist level. Staple the webbing to the box at a 45-degree angle and fill the tray with pint boxes. It's great for picking raspberries or blackberries—you can use both hands.
—*Doraine and Mary Paysinger*
*Salem, Arkansas*

**Use a large** mixing spoon with a good handle to dig up new potatoes. —*Gloria Porter Grandin, North Dakota*

**When I plant** summer bulbs, such as gladiolus, I put a Popsicle stick in the ground near each bulb. If the bulbs haven't sprouted when I start setting out bedding plants later, I know where I can and can't dig. —*Mary Lancaster Pikeville, North Carolina*

plants from freezing at night. The extra heat speeds up growth even if there's no threat of frost. I get tomatoes 2 weeks before my neighbors.
—*Jane Lasley*
*Raleigh, North Carolina*

**Plastic milk jugs** cut into strips make excellent plant markers. The jugs are also useful as collars to keep pill bugs and worms from destroying young plants.
—*Pamela Shelburne*
*Wilson, Oklahoma*

**Make scoops** from old bleach bottles or milk jugs by cutting off the bottom and one side up to the handle. They make perfect tools for scooping potting soil, peat moss, birdseed and compost. Actually, the uses are endless.
—*Gail Russell*
*Reiman Publications*

**When I** sent my son out to pick raspberries, he came up with a wonderful idea. He cut the top off a gallon plastic milk jug and put his belt through the handle. That left both of his hands free for picking the berries. Not bad for a 7-year-old gardener.
—*Pat Jarrar*
*Livonia, Michigan*

**I have** a spreading cactus with long sharp spines. After a rain or watering, I use my kitchen tongs to reach in and pull out any weeds that have germinated.
—*Mrs. Richard Nelson, Albion, Nebraska*

**Old pantyhose** make very effective dusters for applying powdered insecticides and fungicides. Cut off a section of nylon to cover the top of the container. Use a rubber band to hold it on tight. Take it to the garden and shake gently for a nice cloud of dust. (Read label directions when using insecticides and fungicides.)
—*Laura Koogler*
*Singers Glen, Virginia*

**To keep** a hanging plant from drying out rapidly, line the pot with a disposable diaper (absorbent side up) and fill with soil and plants. The diaper holds water, then releases it as the soil begins to dry out. Plants stay perky with half as many waterings.
—*Linda Scharer*
*Deerfield, Michigan*

**To keep tall flowers** from falling over, cut a tomato cage into sections with wire cutters, leaving "legs" attached to each circle of wire. Slip the circle around the plant and push the legs into the soil as far as needed.
—*Debbie Hamilton*
*Bel Alton, Maryland*

**Use resealable plastic** bags to save flower seeds before the pods holding them burst open. Just "zip" bags over stems as pods form. Use bags designed for vegetables because they have pin holes in them that allow the seeds to finish drying.

I also use a carpenter's nail bag around my waist to carry yard tools, seed packages and other items while gardening.
—*Anna Mae Ledford*
*Hollywood, Florida*

**Remove** difficult-to-reach residue in bud vases by placing dishwashing liquid, water and a little uncooked rice in the vase and shaking gently. It's much easier to handle than bleach and really effective.
—*Margot King*
*La Grange, Georgia*

**Plastic soft drink bottles** can be cut into long strips 1/2-inch wide for inexpensive plant markers. I use them in the cold frame and when starting plants in the house. They can be moved to the garden, too.
—*Mrs. Harley Andrews*
*Nenzel, Nebraska*

**When rooting** cuttings, put a resealable vegetable bag (the ones with pin holes for ventilation) over the pot of cuttings and "zip" it tight around the pot. It holds just enough moisture for the cuttings to take root.
—*Virginia Becker*
*McHenry, North Dakota*

I have many photos of my flowers, but I didn't know the names of some of the plants I received from friends. So now, whenever I receive a new nursery or seed catalog, I page through it looking for pictures of those mystery plants. When I find one, I cut out the information about the plant and attach it to the back of my photographs for future reference.
—*Dawn Neibarger*
*Mio, Michigan*

I use latex surgical gloves, sold at drugstores, for working in the garden. What a find! My nails and hands stay clean and dry through hours of digging and weeding, but the gloves are thin enough that I don't lose any sense of touch.

I also found they are perfect for hand picking bugs and slugs…I just throw them away when I'm done.
—*Geri Layhon*
*Vashon, Washington*

To remind me what I've planted and when certain plants bloom, I take pictures throughout the growing season with a camera that imprints the date on the photo. These photos help me make needed improvements. For example, I can spot times when my garden lacks color and correct it the following year. And the photos are also a nice record of how my garden has evolved over the years.
—*Leslie Davis*
*Broken Arrow, Oklahoma*

To spread lime on my garden plants, I use a 1-pound coffee can with several holes punched in the bottom. (Use lime sparingly in alkaline soils, also known as "sweet" soils.) Before filling the can, I put the plastic lid on the bottom so the lime doesn't leak out the holes. When the can is filled and I'm ready to dust, I put the lid back on the top.
—*Irene Lynn*
*Smithfield, Pennsylvania*

Instead of buying expensive trellises for my climbing plants, I bought an old decorative wicker screen for $10 and removed the hinges. Now I have three trellises that are quite attractive.
—*Janice Meisner*
*Cottage Grove, Oregon*

To water potted plants easily, stick one end of a thin cotton rope in the soil and the other in a bucket of water.
—*Ann Zawistowski*
*Blaine, Minnesota*

**143**

**Use strips** of carpet or carpet padding to mulch between your garden rows. It keeps the weeds down, allows water to penetrate and lets you walk through the rows when it's wet without getting muddy. At the end of the season, roll up the strips to reuse them the following year.
—*Jane Grabenstein-Chandler*
*Lincoln, Nebraska*

**We lay 2-foot-wide** strips of old carpet around our tomato plants to help prevent blight. It keeps dirt (that may carry the fungus) from splashing on the plants. It also keeps moisture in, weeds out, and it's nice to walk on when picking tomatoes.
—*Deallis Rykhus*
*Garvin, Minnesota*

**If your flowerpot's** drainage holes are too large, line the bottom with netting or an old piece of screen. This allows water to drain out, but keeps the soil from going with it.
—*Cookie Santerre*
*Windham, New Hampshire*

**When I had** an abundance of okra one year, I asked my young sons to help me cut it. To keep the gooey stuff off their hands and arms, they wore old tube socks as gloves. (I used them, too!)
—*Sharleen Worthey, Haslet, Texas*

**Plastic kitchen wrap** twisted into a rope works very well to tie plants to stakes. It doesn't slip, won't cut into tender plants and is economical. If you use green tinted wrap, it becomes almost invisible among your plants. —*Betty Pierce Slaterville Springs, New York*

**Use a potato masher** to rake and break up clumps of soil in your window boxes and large planters.
—*Almira Dombeck*
*Mukwonago, Wisconsin*

**When a spring frost** threatened our garden, we covered the strawberries with old sheets, but didn't have enough for the tomatoes and peppers. So we folded down the tops of brown paper bags and placed them over these plants. We put a little dirt on the folds to keep the bags from blowing away. It saved our plants. —*Janet Huff Mendon, Michigan*

**Old butter knives** from garage sales or secondhand stores are great for small weeding jobs. I keep one in the corner of each flower bed and vegetable garden to save time and steps. —*Eleanor Novak Cleveland, Ohio*

**A child's wagon** is great for transporting flats or pots to the garden.
—*Alice Rae Nelson*
*Beloit, Wisconsin*

**We have** tall flowering plants, like hollyhocks and cosmos, that must be tied to a fence or they'll be flattened by the wind. We've tried wire ties, but they damage the plants. Twine, string and fabric ties don't hold up well to our weather, and

**To kill dandelions** in my strawberry patch, I cut both ends from a 2-liter bottle, place it over the weed and spray with Roundup (or other total vegetation killers that *do not* stay in the soil). This keeps the herbicide off the strawberries.

*—Ralph Summers*
*Mountain Grove, Missouri*

the rain makes any knots impossible to untie in fall.

Our solution is 3/16-inch clear vinyl tubing sold at hardware stores for about 10¢ a foot. It's strong, nearly invisible and unaffected by weather. A single knot at each end grips like a bulldog, yet is easily undone. The tubing can be used year after year and won't damage even the most delicate plants.

*—Wayne Norton*
*Ridgeville, Indiana*

**Cut up old pantyhose** to tie up your tomatoes. They're soft and won't cut into the plant.

*—M. Nichols, Cleveland, Ohio*

**I save** and thoroughly rinse empty spray bottles that held household cleaners. Then I use them to mix and apply weed killer. Be sure to label the bottles with their new contents.

*—George Le Gore*
*York, Pennsylvania*

**To walk** among zucchini, pumpkin, watermelon and cucumber plants without stepping on their leaves, I place a path of empty shoe boxes and crates throughout the garden in spring. The leaves grow thickly around the boxes, but I just step *into* each box to walk through the garden.

*—Pauline Fender*
*Coloma, Michigan*

**I use side rails** from a discarded crib as a trellis for my climbing rose. The rails could also stand teepee-style for peas to climb on. Some older cribs are unsafe for infants because the rails are too far apart, so this is a good way to recycle them.

*—Nancy Reece*
*Mount Laurel, New Jersey*

**I plant tomatoes** on both sides of a snow fence. As they grow, I tie them to the fence instead of using stakes.

*—Clayton Pflug*
*Beaver Falls, Pennsylvania*

**My left-hand** garden gloves wear out fast, leaving me with several good right-hand gloves. I make new left-hand gloves by turning the right-hand ones inside-out. Just grasp the seam inside each finger with needle-nose pliers and pull.

*—Joyce Ryder*
*North Branch, Michigan*

In fall, before putting away garden tools, I wash them with soap and water to disinfect them. Then I apply a light coat of oil.

—*Alice Rae Nelson*
*Beloit, Wisconsin*

Last season, we used orange plastic mesh fencing—the kind contractors use to enclose work areas—to provide support for pole beans. Wood braces were placed every 5 or 6 feet for support. We used twine to tie the 4-foot-tall fence to the braces. It was a lot of work, but it was worth it. We planted beans on both sides of the fence, and you wouldn't believe how nicely they climbed it.

—*Josephine Pachuta*
*Beckley, West Virginia*

Here's a tip for those who freeze or can corn. Take a 4-inch square of pine board and smooth the edges. Drive a long finishing nail into the center. Spear the ear of corn onto the nail so the ear stays upright as you cut off the kernels.

—*Thelma Carpenter*
*Great Bend, Kansas*

To make "wire stakes", use wire cutters to remove the curved top of a coat hanger. Divide the rest in half so two V-shaped pieces remain. Squeeze the sides of each "V" together and use these handy devices to secure dripper hoses, chicken wire covers for spring flowers, plastic cup covers for seedlings, etc.
—*Michelene Rocco, Lemont, Illinois*

My favorite homemade tool for cleaning the insides of dry gourds is a shish kebab skewer about 10 inches long. I put a cork on the pointed end and use the rounded end to loosen the seeds. Then I shake the seeds out. It's great when making birdhouses from gourds.

—*Crystal White*
*Chesterton, Indiana*

Use baseball bat tape to wrap tool handles for a better grip—and no more splinters. —*Suzie McIntire*
*Paola, Kansas*

I bought a small outdoor garbage can with wheels to hold the seed-starting mix I make at home. I can mix everything together right in the can. It also can be moved easily and is great for storage.

—*Jodie Stevenson*
*Export, Pennsylvania*

I like to save seeds from my flowers. But when they're done blooming, it's hard to remember what color they were. So I write the color on a small white tag from a bread bag and attach it to a stem while it's still in bloom. This helps me identify the color later.

—*Rose Krushelniski*
*Nipawin, Saskatchewan*

Antique wagon wheels make great trellises for just about any climbing plant. —*Neta Liebscher*
*El Reno, Oklahoma*

**My pole beans** and cucumbers grow on trellises, but our rocky clay soil makes it tough to drive the supporting legs in securely. Stakes and ropes from an old tent made ideal braces. My reinforced trellises have withstood several thunderstorms and even a hurricane.
*—Barbara Dege*
*Hackensack, New Jersey*

**I use wooden shims** bought at a lumber yard to mark plants, support drooping vines and hold down plastic weed barriers. The shims are thin at one end, so they can be pushed into the ground effortlessly.
*—Doris Gish, Remer, Minnesota*

**A shoehorn** is useful for loosening soil or digging small holes when transplanting. *—Diane Hutchinson*
*Tillsonburg, Ontario*

**To keep** your water garden plants in place, fill old pairs of pantyhose with pebbles and place them at the top of the plants' pots. This helps sink the plants and keep them in place. *—Ann Ward*
*Naples, Florida*

**I put a bar of soap** in a mesh bag, then tie it on or near the outside faucet. It's a great way to get your hands clean after gardening—and you won't have to search for the soap. *—Suzie McIntire*
*Paola, Kansas*

**I save** large brown plastic coffee-creamer jars to store my dried flowers and petals. I keep them separated by color until I decide what mixture I need for a particular craft.
*—Valerie Evanson*
*Phoenixville, Pennsylvania*

**I use** 12-inch pipe cleaners from the craft store to tie tomatoes and other plants to stakes. They're easy to use, and the soft chenille won't hurt the plants. They're also reusable and last several years.
*—Mary Ann Richards*
*Chicago, Illinois*

**My husband** made me a weeding tool that I use often. He took an old screwdriver, bent about 1 inch of the end at a right angle to form an "L" and sharpened both sides. It's very nice for weeding new plants or small spaces and has a nice handle as well.
*—Marlene Smalldridge*
*Princeton, Idaho*

**I made** inexpensive stepping stones by filling a springform cake pan with cement. Before it dried, I had my children make a hand or foot print in each. Then I used magnetic alphabet letters to imprint each child's name and the date. We plan to add new stepping stones to our yard each year.
*—Mary Schmidt*
*Hawarden, Iowa*

**My chopsticks** work great for making holes for onion sets and certain seeds. Dragging a chopstick through the dirt creates a perfect trench for planting seeds.

—*Mary Ohms, Carrollton, Texas*

**When I plant seeds** or set out plants, I write the name of each item on a piece of paper, then put it in a small clear plastic jar to mark the location. —*Joyce Ryder North Branch, Michigan*

**I save marigold seeds** every fall. After frost, I pull up a few plants to dry. To identify the color, I clip a clothespin to a stem and write the color of the plant on the clothespin with permanent marker. After gathering the dried seeds, I clip the clothespins to the containers they're stored in. —*Mrs. Vic Wittrock Halbur, Iowa*

**Bleach** will disinfect garden equipment, pots, etc. Use 2 tablespoons of bleach per quart of water.
—*Becky Gore, Evansville, Indiana*

**To plant** tiny carrot seeds, put them in an empty seasoning container— the kind with a removable sifter top. Put tape over half of the holes, then gently shake down the row. The seeds are planted in no time, and the carrots will need little, if any, thinning. —*Pearl Henderson Baldwin, Wisconsin*

**I collect colorful** plastic spoons from Dairy Queen treats to mark garden rows. For fun, you can even coordinate the color to the crop— yellow for corn, red for radishes, white for onions, etc.
—*Laura Leinen Doran, Minnesota*

**I use** 5-quart plastic ice cream buckets in the garden. They're handy for picking produce, storing tools, carrying compost and storing seed packets. Since they're free when you buy ice cream, it's no great loss if one breaks or gets messy. —*Deborah Moyer Liberty, Pennsylvania*

**I use old spoons** from garage sales to dig and plant bulbs, seeds and small plants. They're less expensive and much easier for me to handle than other garden tools.
—*Ann Ward, Naples, Florida*

**Top tomato cages** with an empty 8-, 10- or 12-inch pot—whatever size fits. Then use it at planting time to hold seed packets, garden tools and plant markers. It can easily be moved around the garden so it's always near where you are working.
—*Ruth Ann Potter Grand Rapids, Michigan*

---

### Tip from Our "Landlady"

*In fall, cut healthy pest-free annual flowers with a mulching mower and then till everything into the soil. Your soil will be rich and ready for planting in the spring.* —*Gail Russell Reiman Publications*

---

**To save time** when mulching around transplants, cover each plant with a plastic cup. Pour mulch over entire bed, cups included, to a depth of 2 to 3 inches. Then simply lift the cups off the plants.

—*Diane Hutchinson*
*Tillsonburg, Ontario*

**Draw tulips** on a gallon bleach bottle and cut them out. Punch two holes in the center of each tulip— one near the top, the other near the bottom. Cut curved ends off a coat hanger, slip it through the holes and mark where you've planted bulbs. —*Sibyl Brian*
*Oklahoma City, Oklahoma*

**Use this** mini-greenhouse to protect delicate seedlings. Buy 12-ounce clear plastic cups and puncture one side. Place over the plant, securing at least one side with wire. For larger plants, cut the top off a 2-liter clear plastic bottle, invert over plant and attach to a wooden stake to keep the wind from blowing it away. —*Michelene Rocco*
*Lemont, Illinois*

**Old tomato cages** make perfect flower supports. You can use them whole for large plants, like peonies, or cut them apart and use each leg by itself. —*Ruth Ann Potter*
*Grand Rapids, Michigan*

**An old fondue fork** is perfect for loosening small weeds around young plants. —*Mary Ellen Howe*
*Mitchell, Oregon*

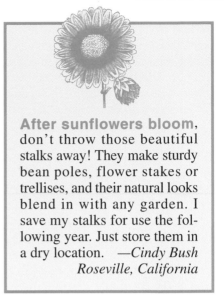

**After sunflowers bloom**, don't throw those beautiful stalks away! They make sturdy bean poles, flower stakes or trellises, and their natural looks blend in with any garden. I save my stalks for use the following year. Just store them in a dry location. —*Cindy Bush*
*Roseville, California*

**I plant extra** tomato seeds so we can give seedlings to friends and coworkers. To transport them, we cut a 2- or 3-liter soft drink bottle in half, insert the plant and use clear tape to reseal the bottle.

—*Laurie Gehrt*
*Broken Arrow, Oklahoma*

**For a simple** no-fuss garden, we put plywood over a wagon and set three pots of tomatoes on top. On hot summer days, and when we had hail in September, we just rolled our "garden" under the patio overhang.

—*The Copland family*
*Concord, California*

**To save space**, put one large tomato cage atop another and tie them together. Put tomato stakes inside for extra support. Cucumbers or melons will climb all the way to the top. —*Phillip Maiorana*
*Ashford, Connecticut*

**When my husband** threw away an old boat cushion, I cut it open and found four of the nicest knee pads. They're filled with soft stuffing and covered in heavy plastic—just right for kneeling on wet grass.
—*Joyce Nichols, Elida, Ohio*

**A paper coffee filter** is a big improvement over stones and broken pottery for covering drainage holes in flowerpots. Soil won't wash out of the bottom. —*Pauline Chandler Hemet, California*

**Lids from** 6- and 12-ounce juice cans make plant markers that really hold up to weather and dirt. Make a hole in each lid and write the plant name with an oil-based paint marker. Cut wire coat hangers to the desired length and insert one end in the lid hole and the other in the ground.
—*Linda Chartrant Milan, Ohio*

**For plant labels**, cut a lightweight 5-quart ice cream pail into several strips with pointed ends and write on them with a permanent marker. They'll last several years.
—*Gloria Porter Grandin, North Dakota*

**When my husband** found an old metal bed frame discarded alongside a country road, I turned it into a trellis for my Lady Banks rose.
—*Gay Nicholas, Henderson, Texas*

**A potato peeler** is handy for digging up tiny seedlings and moving them. —*Mary Stager Silver Bay, Minnesota*

**If you collect seeds**, place them in plastic 35mm film containers. They're airtight, unbreakable and just the right size for tiny seeds.
—*Marion King Gloucester, Ontario*

**Here's a neat trellis** for pole beans. Sink a 7- to 8-foot (1/2-inch round) water pipe into the ground and mount a bicycle wheel to the top. Tie string from the wheel and stake to the ground. Plant your pole beans by each stake so the plants can climb the lines as they grow. They're beautiful when covered and picking beans is easy. —*Rose King Belleville, Wisconsin*

**I mark rows** by painting the names of flowers and vegetables on smooth flat rocks. A colorful design brightens the garden, and the grandkids love to help.

—*Neta Liebscher*
*El Reno, Oklahoma*

**Need** a watering can? I use an old fabric-softener bottle. I punched holes in the lid and two more in the jug right above the handle to draw in air as water is poured out.

—*Sharon Nolt*
*Bethel, Pennsylvania*

**Before frost**, I pick all my cherry tomatoes and pack them "by the dozen" in egg cartons. The tomatoes don't touch each other, and they're in a dark place with easy access.

—*Debbie Learman, Echo, Oregon*

**Use an old** cracked plastic ice-cube tray to start seeds. Drill a drainage hole in the bottom of each compartment. When seedlings are ready to transplant, just pop out the soil cubes or scoop them out with a fork.

—*Jill Woods*
*Colorado Springs, Colorado*

**If you use** plastic labels to identify cuttings, don't throw them out after one season. Wash the lettering off with a scrubbing pad and reuse them for the next batch.

—*Louise Theriault*
*Waltham, Massachusetts*

**I've tried** writing on plant markers with freezer pens, grease pens and permanent markers, but they all seem to wear off over time. To prevent this, paint over the writing with clear nail polish.

—*Marilyn Fils*
*Creston, Iowa*

**Arthritis** makes it difficult for me to pull weeds, but an old boning knife with a sharp point is a great help. If you're careful, you can use it to transplant seedlings, too.

—*Sharon Bradshaw*
*Richmond, Missouri*

**My garden hoe** is marked at 6-inch intervals, from 6 inches to 3 feet. I use a good paint to make the marks and cover them with 3 layers of polyurethane. I add an extra coat of polyurethane every fall before I store my tools.

—*Betty Nelson*
*Des Moines, Iowa*

**Use a waterproof marker** to write the names of plants on the blades of white plastic knives. Push the handles into the ground. They can be used year after year.

—*Evelyn Iden, Filion, Michigan*

**Cut mini-blind** slats into 8-inch sections to make plant markers. I write on them with pencil, which seems to last longer than permanent marker.

—*Carole Bergman*
*Anderson, South Carolina*

**White flour** comes in handy when I want an edge marked for cutting or spraying in the grass.

—*Valerie Giesbrecht*
*Othello, Washington*

151

**I use a spark plug** wrench to uproot weeds in my ground cover. The screwdriver part gets under and loosens the weed, and the wrench part fits nicely in the palm of my hand for leverage. My husband had to buy a new one because his original wrench is now in my garden toolbox. *—Alta Thompson*
*Waldport, Oregon*

**I got tired** of walking to the shed for my watering can and other assorted garden tools. So I cut the branches off a dead cedar tree, sunk the trunk in a hole filled with cement and treated it with water seal. Then I added plenty of hooks and holders to hang my things.
*—Shawna Landy, Valley View, Texas*

**Spray paint** the handles of your garden tools florescent colors. They'll be easy to locate in your flower beds. *—Carole Bergman*
*Anderson, South Carolina*

**When I misplaced** my knee pad, I had to find a replacement quickly. So I cut my grandchildren's swimming pool toy, called a "noodle", into two 12-inch pieces. Then I cut them once lengthwise to open the tube. I tied them to my knees with shoestrings. This worked even better than my old cushion.
*—Louise Harrison*
*Anderson, South Carolina*

**An old broom handle** with a nail inserted into the bottom end is a perfect litter picker. File the nail head to a point. This helps me keep my beds and borders clean of windblown leaves and trash. It also saves my back. *—Cornelius Hogenbirk*
*Waretown, New Jersey*

**Use a two-tined kitchen fork** to help repot plants. Just poke the fork into the roots and give a gentle

**Sew an old pair** of shoulder pads inside the legs of your jeans right by each knee. This way you don't have to keep moving a kneeling pad.
*—Maxine Alm*
*Wauwatosa, Wisconsin*

twist. This loosens the roots without damaging them. It is also helpful when plants are root bound.

—*Dorothy Doll*
*Rancho Palos Verdes, California*

**Use garbage twist-ties** to help train vines to grow up a fence or trellis. Be sure to twist the ties loosely so there's plenty of room for the vines to grow.  —*Amber Wall*
*Hawthorne, Florida*

**To help tomatoes** get a good start, I place tin cans with the tops and bottoms cut out on a tray. I'll fill the cans 1/3 full of potting soil and then place one plant in each. Then I'll add more potting soil and firm. After a week or so, when the plants are established, I plant the cans (with the plants in them) in the garden. Then I'll pull each can up about 1/3 of the way to help protect the plants from cutworms.

—*Della Rebbe, Fremont, Nebraska*

**Mark perennial** plants with wooden shish kebab sticks at the end of the growing season. That way in spring, you won't mistake them for weeds.  —*Marilyn Carter*
*Brimley, Michigan*

**I've found** the perfect tool for digging in our rocky Missouri soil—my husband's long-handled screwdriver. It's great for prying and dislodging any size rock.

—*Ginny George, Neosho, Missouri*

**Keep** your garden tools from rusting. Keep a roll of paper towels and

a can of WD40 lubricant nearby. When you finish deadheading or planting, spray some of the oil onto a paper towel and wipe the tools.

—*Mary Isaacsen-Bright*
*Los Osos, California*

**An old** kitchen knife and fork are ideal garden tools. A fork can lift seedlings without breaking the roots, and it's perfect for cultivating or weeding in planters. A knife is just the right size for separating a flat full of plants.  —*Barbara Dege*
*Hackensack, New Jersey*

**I believe** in fixing something that breaks or making another use for it. That's just what I did with the broken handle of a spatula. It works great for planting, weeding and a variety of other garden tasks.

—*Gabrielle Litzenberg*
*Chadron, Nebraska*

**Use twist-ties** from bread bags to mark the stems of particularly beautiful flowers. Then you can save the seeds from these flowers to plant next year.  —*Laura Leinen*
*Doran, Minnesota*

**To protect plants** from cutworms, I remove the top and bottom from 1/2-gallon juice cans and place them over my plants. I also conserve water by filling the can each time I water. This directs the water right to the root area.  —*Pat Greathead*
*Westminster, Maryland*

**Nylon stockings** make great storage bags for bulbs. The bulbs receive plenty of air. And they can be dipped in pesticide, then allowed to drain and dry right in the stocking. (Label the stockings if bulbs are treated with pesticides.)
*—Louise Theriault*
*Waltham, Massachusetts*

**When painting** concrete blocks around a flower bed, use a sponge instead of a brush. It will fill the tiny holes in the blocks better and faster.
*—Ruth Patterson*
*Maridianville, Alabama*

**To keep shoes** dry and clean, place a plastic grocery bag on each foot and tie them around your ankles with the handles. When finished, throw the bags out.
*—A.R. Capalupo, Utica, New York*

**Use old soft drink bottles** to water your plants and save your back. These are much lighter than a watering can. *—R. King*
*Monticello, Florida*

**For small weeding jobs**, I slip a plastic bag on each arm and secure with a rubber band. I can grip the weeds better, and if I accidentally find poison ivy, I don't have to worry. I just turn the bags inside-out as I take them off. *—Marie Mumman*
*Somerdale, New Jersey*

**To help keep** a shepherd's crook holding bird feeders or hanging baskets straight, insert a 1/2-inch galvanized pipe that's about 18 inches

**After years** of bruising and pounding my fingers while cracking hickory nuts with a hammer, my son came up with a great suggestion. "Use your vise," he said. It works great. After a little practice, the nut meats now come out in perfect halves. *—Catharine Binnig*
*Thompson, Ohio*

long into the ground. Sink it in straight until the top is about an inch or so below the surface (to avoid damage to a mower blade). Slide the crook inside the pipe and enjoy its nice straight display. (If underground utility wires are used in your yard, call your utility company before sinking the pipe.)
*—Stan Merrill, St. Paul, Minnesota*

**Use Avon's** Silicone Glove on your hands before gardening. They will wash clean and be soft afterward. *—Helen Condon*
*Carlisle, Pennsylvania*

**I use old tires** to make raised flower beds. Take a roofing or utility knife and remove one sidewall of the tire by cutting near the tread. (There's no wire in the sidewall of a tire, so it should cut pretty easily.) Then place the tire upside-down. It helps keep plants moist and their leaves off the ground.
*—Naomi Ochs*
*Independence, Missouri*

# CHAPTER FIFTEEN

# THE INSIDE SCOOP

MANY PEOPLE enjoy gardening indoors as well as outdoors.

Besides providing adequate light and proper water and fertilizer, here are a few suggestions to make caring for your houseplants a snap.

We're confident your windowsill gardens will be as lush and green throughout the year as your outdoor garden plants are during the warm season.

**If your hanging plants** drip water, get an extra spring-loaded shower curtain rod. Hang it over the middle of the tub. Now you can water the plants and let them drip in the tub. *—Kim Van Horsen Monrovia, California*

**Every time** I water my houseplants, including my prized bonsai, I rotate the pot a quarter turn. This way new growth comes up evenly, and the plants do not lean in search of light. *—Judy Larson Greendale, Wisconsin*

**For hassle-free** African violets, use wire or an ice pick to thread a 1-inch strip of fabric (cotton works well) through the bottom of the pot and up through the soil. Poke the other end of the fabric through the lid of a plastic margarine tub. Fill the tub with water, put on the lid and set the plant on top of the lid. I add fertilizer to the water when I fill the tubs. *—Rita Harper Orange Park, Florida*

**Rub mayonnaise** on the leaves of your houseplants to clean them and make them shine. *—Peggy Ratliff North Tazewell, Virginia*

**I move** my Christmas cactus outside during the summer. But to brighten it up when it's not blooming, I plant impatiens with it. Outdoors, the impatiens bloom beautifully. When I bring the plants in, the impatiens take a rest, and the cactus begins blooming.

It seems the impatiens leave just enough water for the cactus to thrive. *—Barbara Petersen Colorado Springs, Colorado*

**Here's how** I keep small houseplants moist while on vacation. For each plant, I punch a few small holes in a plastic bag. I enclose each plant in a bag and fasten with a twist-tie after watering. The plants stay moist for up to a few weeks. *—Lucille Ruth Port Charlotte, Florida*

**Try watering** hanging plants with ice cubes. As the ice melts, the soil absorbs the water, and it doesn't drip out of the bottom of the pot. *—Roslyn Francis, Lodi, California*

**Use coffee grounds** and leftover coffee on your houseplants and watch them thrive. I've been doing this for a long time, and it really works. *—Delores Koland Pelican Rapids, Minnesota*

**When plant leaves** get dusty, clean them with a rag dipped in

**To stop the drips** of indoor hanging baskets, I buy plastic planters the same diameter as my original basket but without drain holes. I remove the chains from my original basket and attach them to the new container after drilling three holes near the rim. Then the original basket is placed into the new container, using foam packing "peanuts" or other material to separate the pots. (This keeps the plants from sitting in water.) I occasionally have to empty water that collects in the new container.—*Bonita Laettner*
*Angola, New York*

milk. It leaves them shiny and is much cheaper than buying commercial sprays. —*Diane Lee*
*Richland Center, Wisconsin*

**The simple secret** to helping your Christmas cactus rebloom is to cut back on watering come fall. Place the cactus in a cool spot and water it only after the well-drained potting mix dries out.

I also keep mine in a cool spot during the daytime.

—*Ruth Waterman*
*Newport Beach, California*

**I couldn't** throw away the poinsettia my son gave me in 1991. So I came up with a way to keep it thriving and blooming just at the right time.

After the holidays, I keep it in a corner of the house near a sunny window. I plant it in my rock garden in spring when the temperature remains about 50°, placing the plant (pot and all) in a semi-shaded area. I bring it back in the house on the first day of autumn.

Then I use a procedure I call "long night/short day" to get it to bloom again. I keep it in complete darkness for 14 continuous hours each night. (Either move it to a dark room, closet or put a box over it.) Continue this treatment for 8 to 10 weeks. It will be beautiful for Christmas! —*Loretta Coverdell*
*Amanda, Ohio*

**Use room-temperature** or warm water when watering houseplants. This prevents them from going into shock (especially the young ones).

—*Darlene Wyness*
*Williams Lake, British Columbia*

**Save your pencil shavings.** Spread them around houseplants to help keep aphids and mites at bay.

—*Judith Umberger*
*Hurricane, West Virginia*

# CHAPTER SIXTEEN

# A BUSHEL OF BITS

WE RECEIVED so many good tips for this garden secrets book that we didn't know where to put all of them.

So please bear with us…in this chapter we've lumped together a potpourri of hints and ideas that just didn't seem to fit anywhere else. In the following pages, you'll learn what plants will attract birds and butterflies to your yard, tips to keep water gardens blooming, ideas to keep young gardeners' hands busy, how to keep cut flowers fresh looking, and much more.

**I planted** a short row of ever-bearing strawberries, some ever-bearing red raspberries and a few blueberry bushes in my garden. The children love searching out these nourishing treasures. —*Lori Lyles*
*Middlebury, Indiana*

**I volunteer** at our school, helping students plant vegetable and flower gardens. We plant seed potatoes in a large plastic container every March 17. In late April, each student has a potato plant to take home. We plant some in the school garden, too, and dig the mature potatoes for the students to take home in September to enjoy with a meal.
—*Catherine Bleem, Sparta, Illinois*

**Four-o'clocks** are good flowers for children to grow. These brightly colored annuals grow 2 to 3 feet tall and have fragrant blooms that open and close. My grandmother always had them, and I loved watching them. —*Dot Weber*
*Longview, Texas*

**My parents**, who were avid gardeners, divided our garden into four parts—one big plot for the family and a smaller one for each of their three children. We drew up our own plans, chose and planted seeds, weeded and harvested our own plots. Now that I have my own garden, I do the same for my daughters. They love to help. —*Katie Vandergriff*
*Powell, Tennessee*

**Children love** to plant gardens. Help them make a "salad garden" by plotting a circle at least 6 feet across. Plant one staked or caged tomato in the center, then make "spokes" with rows of onions and plant a different vegetable in each section.

You can add a couple of marigolds for color. As you harvest your garden, plant more seeds right away so it continues to produce.
—*Susie Fisher*
*Lewistown, Pennsylvania*

**When pumpkins** are small, carefully write each child's name in the skin with a sharp pencil. As the pumpkin grows, so does the name. It doesn't hurt the pumpkin, and children of all ages enjoy seeing their names get bigger and bigger.
—*Mary Cay Dinning*
*Bonners Ferry, Idaho*

**To get kids interested** in gardening, don't forget to plant radishes and lettuces. They grow fast and give quick results while waiting for other plants to sprout or bloom.

—*Melinda Myers*
*Milwaukee, Wisconsin*

**Always leave** a corner of your garden where little ones can play, build "roads" or just dig. This way, you can keep an eye on them while you hoe. Remember, kids love to help, too. After helping me pick green beans, my grandson ate some—for the first time!

—*Neva Mathes, Pella, Iowa*

**My children** are too little to do much in the garden, so I give them extra seeds to plant in clear bowls. They can see not only the growing plants, but also what goes on beneath the soil surface. Be sure to place seeds at the edge of the bowl so the roots will be visible.

—*Elizabeth Srutowski*
*Mesa, Arizona*

**For a fun playhouse** that kids will love, make a tepee with poles or long branches, leaving a 2-foot opening as a door. Plant edible Scarlet Runner beans outside and lay clean straw inside for a floor. Water the beans, and the playhouse will grow right before your eyes.

—*Mary Cay Dinning*
*Bonners Ferry, Idaho*

**A "bean hut"** makes a shady hideout and playhouse. We arranged 12 flexible saplings into a 6-foot circle, buried the large ends and secured the tips with twine. Then we wove grapevines through the "walls", leaving a space for a door, and planted pole beans and morning glories at the base of the saplings. The walls blossomed and produced vegetables throughout the summer.

—*Laura Anderson*
*River Falls, Wisconsin*

**We got our son interested** in gardening at an early age by giving him $1 to buy his own seeds, then letting him work the soil and plant them. He sometimes dug them up and replanted them all in the same day, but we let him do things his way. We knew that some of the seeds would eventually grow—and they did. It was a satisfying experience for all of us. —*Connie Moore*
*Medway, Ohio*

**A long-handled** windshield scraper makes a handy tool for brushing snow from bird feeders in winter. It works especially well on platform-type feeders.

—*Lynne McLernon*
*Lake Geneva, Wisconsin*

**If you grow** common milkweed, you'll be rewarded with the beautiful sight of monarch butterfly caterpillars during summer. —*Marlene Condon*
*Crozet, Virginia*

**Keep ants out** of your hummingbird feeder by hanging it on 15-pound-test fishing line. Attach with a metal ring or hook. Just don't let the line or feeder touch the tree trunk or any leaves.
—*Marjorie Walls*
*Hiawassee, Georgia*

**I grow** huge sunflowers to feed the birds. I cut off the heads and dry them. When winter comes, I set whole heads in the trees. It's a feast for the birds. —*Rose Krushelniski*
*Nipawin, Saskatchewan*

**Last year**, we put a new plant near our birdbath. We put a tomato cage over the plant to encourage upright growth. Even though the plant didn't survive, the cage still stands. The birds love to perch on it, often preening themselves there after their bath. —*Steven Lenart*
*St. Clair Beach, Ontario*

**Hummingbirds** use thistle and dandelion fluff to line their nests. They're also attracted—as are butterflies—to Mexican sunflowers, marigolds, periwinkle, lantana, cosmos, morning glories and impatiens. The giant black swallowtail butterfly also likes parsley.
—*Louise Grant*
*Fort White, Florida*

**While a birdhouse** gourd is still growing, scratch in a name with a ball-point pen. As the gourd grows,

the name does, too. When completely cured, cut a hole for a personalized birdhouse.
—*Roberta Witteman, Nampa, Idaho*

**My husband** built a 12-inch-square platform and set it above our tomato plants, then enticed the cardinals to it with sunflower seeds. There were no worms eating the plants or tomatoes—apparently the cardinals took them to feed their young. —*Jean Halma*
*Hudsonville, Michigan*

**Montana bluets** and zinnias are among the American goldfinches' favorite foods. The birds bend the drying flower heads down when they land on them, then pull out the seeds with their bills. It's fascinating to watch. —*Charlene Margetiak*
*Norwalk, Ohio*

**In my garden**, the hummingbirds enjoy morning glories, four-o'clocks, orange-red gladiola, perennial sweet peas, lantana, Turk's cap lily and red hardy glads. —*Marsha Melder*
*Shreveport, Louisiana*

**I hang gourd** birdhouses in my garden to encourage birds to stay.
—*Rita Jemison*
*Ashland, Mississippi*

**To help visualize** your garden plot, mark the outline with a garden hose or rope. Then fill the area with different sized bulky objects (such as lawn bags of leaves) to give you an idea of what your finished garden will look like.
—*Angela Griffin Hatchett*
*Altoona, Alabama*

just as suitable for gardeners in wheelchairs. —*Shirley Harper*
*Spokane, Washington*

**Starting a new** flower bed or planting a tree in sod? Place four to six layers of newspaper over the planting area and anchor it down with rocks and topsoil. Leave it in place 10 to 14 days. The grass will die, and the soil can be dug more easily. —*Jean Jungst*
*Garfield, Minnesota*

**Hummingbirds like** my cypress vines, roses and gladiolus, as well as squash, pumpkin and cucumber flowers. They seem to go for anything yellow or red. I plant lots of sunflowers for them, too.
—*Rita Jemison*
*Ashland, Mississippi*

**Because I have** arthritis, I needed to find an easier way to garden. My husband built a planter box that's about 11 inches deep and as long and wide as the wooden bench it sits on.

It has a series of drainage holes in the bottom. I place coffee filters over the holes, then fill the planter with soil. I've planted tomatoes, beans, carrots, cucumbers, zucchini, petunias and sweet peas in it—all at once! On another bench I have large containers of herbs, lettuces and green onions.

We keep the benches right outside the back door so they're easy to get to. I garden from a chair next to the bench, so I think it would be

**To extend** your garden's "season", preserve flowers and leaves using a flower press or any large heavy book.

Ferns press well, as do coreopsis, violets, Queen Anne's lace, delphinium, phlox, salvia, buttercups and pansies.

It's easy to do. Just pick flowers when they're dry and cut the stems just below the blossoms. Then  lay flowers upside-down on blotting paper or white typing paper. Cover with another sheet of paper and tighten the press or close the book. (Use several sheets of paper when using a book to avoid damaging its pages.) Flowers should be dry in 2 to 3 weeks.

Dried flowers and leaves can be used to decorate pillar candles or they can be glued onto heavy paper and framed.

Other popular crafts include

bookmarks, stationery and greeting cards. To make them yourself, simply glue flowers onto paper and cover with clear Con-Tact paper. They're easy to do, inexpensive and they make great gifts.

*—Judy Hoolsema*
*Portage, Michigan*

I enjoy the foliage of snow-on-the-mountain, but it was spreading throughout my garden. So I removed the top and bottom from a coffee can, buried it so the top was a bit above ground level and set the plant inside. This beautiful bushy plant has been "in the can" for 3 years now and shows no signs of wanting out! *—Sheila Rasmussen*
*Independence, Iowa*

If you entertain in your yard in the evenings, plant white flowers. They show up well, especially in the moonlight. *—Marlene Hooper*
*Mesa, Arizona*

I recycle large coffee cans and use them as flower pots. (If I plant right in the can, I make sure to drill drainage holes in the bottom first.) I spray paint them and sometimes add painted scenes or decals. They're especially nice to use when giving a plant as a gift. *—Ann Ward*
*Naples, Florida*

Before weeding, I remove my rings and cover my hands (including cuticles and the area under my fingernails) with petroleum jelly. Then I wipe off the excess with paper towels. This keeps my hands soft and stain-free when weeding…and cleanup is a breeze.

*—Bernie Decker, Ashland, Ohio*

Place old rubber-backed carpet, rubber side up, between garden rows of annuals and vegetables (not perennials) when planting. It keeps out weeds, is much less messy after a rain, provides a soft surface to kneel on and can be thrown out at the end of the season.

Most carpet installers have plenty of used carpet they'll give you for free. *—Barb Wagner*
*Willmar, Minnesota*

It gets hot here in summer. To keep cool while doing garden chores, I work on the north side of the house in the morning when it's shady. In evening, when the south side of the house is in shade, I work there. *—Paul Peterson*
*Redding, California*

If you have the room and the climate to grow bamboo, you'll have free home-grown materials for plant stakes and tepees for pole beans and tomatoes.

*—Pamela Shelburne*
*Wilson, Oklahoma*

For homes without downspouts, set a wooden barrel at a corner. This softens the flow of water when it rains and collects rainwater for later use. *—Sue Cate*
*Ravenden Springs, Arkansas*

**I keep** a file folder and a big manila envelope next to my plant books to store newspaper and magazine clippings, tips from friends and neighbors and my own gardening ideas.
—*Monica Bengston*
*Independence, Iowa*

**To design** a landscape, jot down the area's measurements and existing trees, shrubs, walks, etc. Transfer the information to 1/8-inch graph paper (1 square equals 1 foot) and make several copies. Note the features you want in your yard, such as a birdbath, pond, paths, etc., until you have a working plan. Make a list of the trees and plants you'd like to add. Then place them on your graph, considering their light requirements, heights, textures and colors. (You may need to refer to a gardening book or ask a nursery professional to help you with this step.)
—*Paul Peterson*
*Redding, California*

**Whenever** you cut wood, take a plastic bag along to collect the sawdust. Since it packs, you can use it for foot paths in your garden.
—*Marie McClure*
*Orangevale, California*

**To press flowers**, place them alphabetically in used phone books—roses under "R", etc.
—*Josephine Slemmons*
*Jackson, Michigan*

**For a pretty display**, place dried flowers in a bottle, pour in oil and seal. —*Elizabeth Srutowski*
*Mesa, Arizona*

**"Wash away"** insect bites with a wet bar of soap. Do not rinse off. Within minutes, you won't even remember you were bitten. I've used this remedy for over 30 years. It works on bee stings, too.
—*Audrey Weinmann*
*Winona, Minnesota*

**When I got tired** of mowing around two telephone poles and three guy wires, I planted flowers around them. I started with daylilies,

---

**I keep notes** on my garden every year—what plants thrived in what types of weather, where everything was, what varieties did well and which ones tasted best. This helps me choose what I want to plant the following year. I also make a "map" of the garden each year, which helps me rotate my crops each spring.
—*Sandy McKenzie*
*Braham, Minnesota*

*Irises did better on the east side of the house.*

*Save seeds from the hot red peppers— Exceptional!*

*Divide hostas... give extras to friends*

*Plant peas 2 weeks earlier*

164

then added daffodil bulbs and geraniums. I have blooms from early spring until frost. The mulched bed is very easy to care for, and I can run my lawn mower around it easily. —*Bonnie Murphy Cincinnati, Ohio*

**To sprout** soft-coated seeds more quickly, place them in a wide-mouthed vacuum bottle with warm water and soak for 24 hours before planting. The water will stay warm, and the seeds can be removed from the bottle easily.
—*Karen Ann Bland, Gove, Kansas*

**Put a jar ring** over small perennials and press it into the ground. Then you can spot tiny plants and not dig them up by mistake.
—*Rosa Cress, Columbiana, Ohio*

**When frost threatens**, we cover flowers and unripe vegetables with old sheets and tablecloths.
—*Marlin Zimmerman Thorp, Wisconsin*

**Selecting** the right plant is critical for good yields and your own gardening enjoyment. Ask your county Extension office what plants grow well in your area. —*Ricky Lewis Jacksonville, Florida*

**I made a garden bench** with a bag of cement, an old flower flat and empty gallon motor-oil jugs. I used the flat for the seat mold and cut the tops off the jugs to make leg molds. When the cement for the seat was set enough, I picked up the filled leg molds and pressed them in to make depressions about 1-3/4 inches deep. The dry cement was easy to remove from the molds. I just turned the seat over and set it atop the legs. —*Darlene Remoehl Klingerstown, Pennsylvania*

**My husband** and I enhanced our backyard pond by threading white Christmas lights through the surrounding rocks. It's beautiful when the sun is setting. —*Jean Shpock Freeland, Pennsylvania*

**Cellophane tape** will remove cactus bristles. If you get a handful of bristles, apply a thin coat of rubber cement, let it dry and rub it off. All the bristles should come right out. —*Rhonda Watson Reedley, California*

**Instead of bringing** fish from our backyard pond inside for winter, I cover the pond with an A-frame made of clear plastic and treated wood. When the temperature drops to 15°, I turn on the recirculating pump. The moving water and greenhouse effect keep the water from freezing, even when the temperature drops to -30°. —*Steven Simpson Pleasantville, Iowa*

**I build ridges** on all the borders of my raised beds to prevent runoff.
—*Luba Davenport, Tully, New York*

**To transplant moss** around a pond, wait for damp rainy weather. Then spread about an inch of light fertile soil in the transplant area. Carefully skim off moss with a spade or flat-edged shovel, then press it into the loose soil. Press soil around edges of the moss to cover any exposed roots. If it's not raining regularly, moisten at least once a day for a couple of weeks.
—*Darlene Remoehl*
*Klingerstown, Pennsylvania*

**Put a big safety pin** on every key ring you have. Then when you work in the yard—or any time you're away from your house or car—use the pin to attach the keys to a pocket so you don't lose them.
—*Mrs. Edward Hopper*
*Kankakee, Illinois*

**To keep hands** soft and clean when working outside, apply hand cream before you start to garden, then put on a pair of inexpensive gloves. —*Irene Gehring*
*Seattle, Washington*

**Share extra** flower seeds by swapping them. We sponsored a swap at our church library that lasted from August through October. I enjoyed sharing my extra seeds and now have new varieties to enjoy next year. —*Yvonne Armstrong*
*Princeton, Kentucky*

**If you're moving** and can't bear to leave your favorite perennials behind, repot them and bury the pots in the garden until it's time to go. (Address this issue in the sales contract.) If you run out of pots, use plastic grocery bags. Punch holes for drainage and bury the filled bags with the handles sticking out of the ground. A bagged plant will keep for several weeks. On moving day, just grab the handles and go.
—*Virginia Gray, Monett, Missouri*

**If you make** a garden path, try planting creeping woolly thyme between the stones. It creates a beautiful pathway, and when you step on the thyme, the scent is wonderful. This plant is very sturdy and can withstand being walked on.
—*Nancy Stoddard*
*Broadus, Montana*

**Keep grocery bags** inside the back door. That way you can slip them over your shoes if you have to go inside for something. This will help keep your floors and carpets

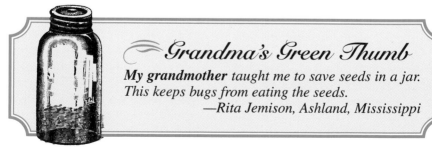

*Grandma's Green Thumb*

**My grandmother** taught me to save seeds in a jar. This keeps bugs from eating the seeds.
—*Rita Jemison, Ashland, Mississippi*

mud free, and you won't have to keep taking your shoes off and putting them back on again.

*—Joe Ricker, Stoughton, Wisconsin*

**I prepared** a 40-foot-square garden bed and installed a stand-pipe sprinkler in the center. I tied a rope to the pipe, walked out about 15 feet, then walked in a circle, trampling down a path so I could lay out my garden in a spoke pattern.

*—David Halbrook*
*Kings Beach, California*

**In summer**, I cook down raspberries and freeze the juice in pre-measured amounts. When I get the "winter blues" in January, I use the frozen juice to make jelly while the snow is blowing. It brings back memories of summer berry-picking and brightens those cold winter days. *—Suzie Newlun*
*Cuba, Illinois*

**Try this mixture** for watering potted plants. Dissolve a package of unflavored gelatin in 1 cup of warm water, then add 2 cups cold water.

*—Monica Bengston*
*Independence, Iowa*

**You can store** seeds for up to 3 years by putting them in their original packets in a jar with some powdered milk. Store in the refrigerator and change the powdered milk every 6 months. *—Louise Theriault*
*Waltham, Massachusetts*

**During** the growing season, I keep a chart showing what I planted and when I planted it, any unusual weather conditions, the size of the harvest and anything else I want to remember. Then in January or February, I take out my records from the previous summer and use that information, along with charts from past years, to help me decide what to plant the next spring.

*—Kathi Richards, Dundee, Ohio*

**Recycle** your Christmas tree—and protect bulbs and perennials at the same time. Cut off branches and lay them in the garden, with the branches overlapping each other about 6 inches. If the soil is soft, push branches in  so they won't blow away. If the ground is frozen, you may need to cover the branches with fine mesh or netting to hold them in place.

*—Rose Marie Casale*
*Hasbrouck Heights, New Jersey*

**In March**, when I start cleaning out garden beds, I fertilize with aged manure. Then I apply compost and spray everything with Miracle-Gro fertilizer until July. The results are excellent. *—Linda Barker*
*Canton, Illinois*

**I plant dill** among my flowers to attract mountain swallowtail butterflies. Bouquet and other short varieties of dill blend in easily. I had swallowtails at all different stages of their life cycle this summer.

*—Jill Woods*
*Colorado Springs, Colorado*

**If you've collected** a number of seashells, place them around the edges of your water garden. We've been amused to see small frogs perching in our shells. We also have seen butterflies, moths and dragonflies drinking from shells where rainwater has collected.
—*Lynn McLernon*
*Lake Geneva, Wisconsin*

**Cut the top off** a plastic 2- or 3-liter soft drink bottle and use the bottom part as a scoop to fill your feeders. Squeeze the soft plastic together when filling to form a spout.
—*Carol Smith*
*Tecumseh, Oklahoma*

**Several years ago**, I planted some wild asters and Mexican sunflowers for the butterflies. When the monarchs start their long trip south, my flowers are just covered with them.
—*Betty Funk*
*Iowa City, Iowa*

**Put a little cucumber** in a small-mouthed jar or bottle while still on the vine and watch it grow inside. When the cucumber nearly fills the jar, cut off at the vine, fill the jar with vinegar and cap it. Everyone will wonder how you managed to get the pickle in the jar.
—*Fannie Miller*
*Montezuma, Georgia*

**This is a good** rainy-day project. Mix about 5 drops of food coloring in 1/4 cup water and pour into a tall glass or bottle. Pick Queen Anne's lace and place it in the container. The flower will absorb the color.
—*Liz McCain, Florence, Oregon*

**To establish ground covers**, such as vinca vine, on a slope or hill, I fashion "hairpins" to coax the plants into going where I want them to be.

I use a pair of bolt cutters to cut off the top part of a clothes hanger. I cut the bottom section into two pieces and bend each into a U-shape. Then I pin the crawling vine "up" the slope instead of down it. Remove the pins once the vine has rooted.
—*Naomi Ochs*
*Independence, Missouri*

**Here's a good way** to transport a vase of cut flowers in the car. Fill a 3-pound coffee can one-third full of heavy gravel. Place the vase in the can and arrange crumpled newspaper around the vase to keep it from falling over.
—*Mrs. Douglas Lopp*
*Thomasville, North Carolina*

**To clean vases** or flower containers that have many small nooks, I use an Efferdent dental cleaning tablet. It works great. I just let it sit and bubble for a few hours, and soon the vase is sparkling. Then I rinse it thoroughly, and it's ready to use again. —*Fran Parr, Eldon, Missouri*

**Plant evergreens** or brightly colored perennials around "eyesores", like heat pumps or air conditioning units, to make them "disappear" into the landscape.
—*Angela Griffin Hatchett*
*Altoona, Alabama*

**Before you work** in the garden, put liquid soap under your fingernails. This makes washing your hands a lot easier.
—*Monica Hutson, Byron, Minnesota*

**To stop birdseed** from sprouting under your feeder, heat it in the microwave oven on high power for 1 minute per cup.    —*Verna Gober*
*Oakridge, Oregon*

**If you don't** have room for a pond, just use a standard washtub. Mine measures 20-by-24 inches and enables me to enjoy the simple pleasures of a pond. I set mine in the ground and used a small pump to create a waterfall that cascades down over stones and into the pond.
—*Nancy Singer*
*Quakertown Pennsylvania*

**Use a large** plastic box, such as those used for mixing cement, to make a small pond. It works great.

Mine's about 24-by-36 inches and approximately 10 inches deep. Just bury it at ground level, edge with flat stones and place flowers around it. Rocks in the middle help birds bathe and drink. —*Charlotte Clark*
*Glenpool, Oklahoma*

**To kill tree stumps** and help them rot fast, I cover them with fresh grass clippings and then with black plastic. It "cooks" the stump.
—*Ernie Staebler*
*Whitewater, Wisconsin*

**In my garden**, zinnias attract all different types of butterflies.
—*Samuel Mott*
*St. Michaels, Maryland*

**Flowers** that attract butterflies include heliotrope, phlox, zinnia, blazing star, butterfly bush, candytuft, Dame's rocket, lavender, stonecrop and sweet William. Thistle attracts both butterflies and goldfinches. Marigolds are popular with most butterfly caterpillars, and the seeds are favorites of goldfinches and sparrows. Swallowtail butterflies raise their young on parsley and carrots.    —*Carol Soehner*
*Centerville, Ohio*

**Don't want the work** of putting up a trellis for pole beans? As early as possible in spring, plant a variety of sweet corn that produces a sizable stalk. At the first sign of a tassel, plant pole beans in the corn row. When you harvest the corn, remove the tassel part and leaves from the stalk to let the sun in. The bean runners will climb the stalks with no additional work on your part. —*C. Orville Delbaugh York, Pennsylvania*

**Plant peas** between your corn plants. The pea vines will use the corn stalks for support.
—*Liz McCain, Florence, Oregon*

**Plant pole beans** next to sunflowers. The beans will climb the lower part of the sunflowers, and you won't need to use any poles.
—*Della Whitesell El Dorado Springs, Missouri*

**I planted my first** "wild garden" by combining seeds I'd collected with three packets of wildflower seeds and dried coffee grounds. I raked the dirt a bit, scattered the seeds with a hand spreader and stepped on them to make sure they had good contact with the soil. The garden was slow getting started, but turned out to be the most enjoyable garden I've ever grown. It seemed like something new bloomed every day. —*Irene Jones Chardon, Ohio*

**To remove** dead leaves from perennial flower beds in spring without damage to plants, use a child's rake to get in among them.
—*Alma Hansen New Denmark, New Brunswick*

**To help** keep cut flowers fresh, add a bit of sugar to the water in the vase. —*Ann Zawistowski Blaine, Minnesota*

**It's easy to read** a rain gauge if you put a few drops of food coloring in the tube. Even if the colored water dries up, there's enough residue to help read the next rainfall amount. —*Karen Ann Bland Gove, Kansas*

**Put cut** flowers in a container of lemon-lime soda mixed with water. They'll last longer.
—*Sharon Walden, Salem, Iowa*

---

### Tip from Our "Landlady"

**When growing** *sweet peas and clematis, plant a low growing flower at its base to shade roots from the hot sun.*
—*Gail Russell Reiman Publications*

---

**Slip plastic** grocery bags over your shoes and tie them around your ankles before heading into a wet yard or garden. I also use these "baggy boots" after mowing so I don't track grass into the house.
—*Dorothy Bower*
*West Alexandria, Ohio*

**Place your old** Christmas tree in the garden and use it as a trellis for climbing beans, peas or cucumbers.
—*Don Telaw, Greendale, Wisconsin*

**Make yourself** a garden bench with a seat that lifts to reveal a deep-storage area for potting soil, leaf bags and garden tools. Besides beautifying your yard and providing a spot for a rest break, it'll save you lots of trips to the tool shed or garage.
—*Dawn Hann*
*Red Hill, Pennsylvania*

**Astilbe has beautiful** colors and grows wonderfully in shade. Snowball bushes work in shady spots, too.
—*Margaret Lindow*
*Suamico, Wisconsin*

**With a small garden**, I'm always trying to find ways to save space. This year I put a tomato cage over my acorn squash plant—it worked great. The plant grew up through the cage, and the squash stayed off the ground.
—*Delia Duprey*
*Oscoda, Michigan*

**We have a catwalk** extending from our second floor. It was dark and dusty underneath until I planted plenty of impatiens. Now this

once-dreary place is bright and cheerful.
—*Rachel Maendel*
*Elka Park, New York*

**We use** plenty of containers and hanging baskets in our cliff-side backyard. We'll add plants with lots of color, but I also like to include plants with all kinds of foliage so the texture is varied.
—*Corinne Hajek*
*LaConner, Washington*

**Spruce up** a narrow shady area with a path made from river rock. It works great at our place in an area where there is only 7-1/2 feet between my house and the neighbor's.

On one side of the path, I planted a shade garden of ferns, hostas and shade-loving herbs. The other side is a mix of other perennials.
—*Elsie Barton , Hoover, Alabama*

**If you save** lots of seeds, store them in labeled plastic containers, like pill bottles, after the seeds are completely dry.
—*Monica Bengston*
*Independence, Iowa*

**We've had** a lot of trees fall down because of storms. So we make use of them by cutting the trunks into slices. They make pretty stepping stones.
—*Deane Taylor*
*Summerfield, North Carolina*

**I love to press** the pretty flowers from my garden. I've found the best time to pick them is from mid-morning to early afternoon to ensure their petals are as dry as possible. That way, the finished product won't look wrinkled.

Also, it is best to press most flowers right after they are picked. Many are so delicate that they start to wilt within just 3 or 4 minutes.
—*Lee Wirth, Mt. Pleasant, Michigan*

**Monarch butterflies** east of the Rocky Mountains migrate to Mexico in fall. To provide nourishment to sustain them as they fly south, I plant goldenrod and lantana as a source of nectar. —*Marlene Condon Crozet, Virginia*

**Don't be reluctant** to stop when you see someone working in their yard to tell them how much you admire their beautiful gardens. Most gardeners are proud to show off their efforts, and some may snip off a piece of plant or offer a seedling for you to take home.
—*Karen Matthews Adams, Massachusetts*

**My 6-year-old** grandson, Derek, grew his own sunflowers. He planted his garden on the side of our garage. After planting, we put screens over them and weighted the corners down with rocks to keep the birds from eating what he'd planted. Our experiment was a success.
—*Allison Pentz Havre de Grace, Maryland*

**When I plant** my amaryllis in the garden come summer, I leave them in pots. Then in fall, I just pull the pots out and bring them in the basement where they lay on their side for 6 to 8 weeks.

Once the bulbs begin to sprout, I plant them in fresh soil, bring them upstairs and place in a bright window. Then I give them a good drink to help start their growing season.
—*Vivian McCorkle Smithville, Missouri*

**I feed** my staghorn fern a mashed banana once a month by carefully working it into the soil. Be careful not to damage the fern's roots.
—*Ann Ward, Naples, Florida*

**Ordinary eggshells** can give your plants a nice early start indoors. Break several so the halves are intact, place them in an empty egg carton, fill the shells with good soil and plant your seeds.

When the weather's warmed and the plants have grown enough to be transplanted, all you have to do is crack the shells around the roots and plant them—shell and all. The shells act as a slow-release natural fertilizer!
—*Glenna Roberts Parkersburg, West Virginia*

**A pointed** mason's trowel is perfect for setting out bedding plants in spring.
—*Rita Christianson Gelburn, North Dakota*

**Roses are** my favorite flowers, but my allergies keep me from bringing the beautiful blooms inside to enjoy. So I plant some near the windows of the rooms where my husband and I spend most of our time. —*Erma Richardson Enumclaw, Washington*

**A neighbor told me** that when you start seeds indoors in pots, it's best to plant them in a small amount of dirt first. Gradually add more dirt as the plant grows.

Do this and your plants will be much stronger and will do better after you transplant them outside. —*Mrs. J.S. Millhouse, Piqua, Ohio*

**Place thoroughly** dried seeds collected from your flower and vegetable gardens in plastic bags. Label, seal and store them in the refrigerator. Come spring, you'll be all set for planting. —*Elsie Kolberg St. Joseph, Michigan*

**Since some plants**—like butterfly bushes—are not reliably hardy in my area, I put them in large pots. When winter comes, I haul them into the garage and water occasionally. My butterfly bush has done well for years. —*Sue Allie Greenfield, Wisconsin*

**Instead of buying** plant stakes, I use small straight limbs that fall from trees. They blend into my gardens and are a lot cheaper. —*Lindy Richee, Burbank, Illinois*

**I often wondered** what the colors of roses represent. I was surprised when I found so many folklore meanings to different colors. Here are some:

- *Red*—Says "I love you" and stands for respect and courage.
- *White*—Conveys reverence, silence and humility.
- *Yellow*—Joy, gladness and friendship.
- *Coral or orange*—Says "Please be mine" and stands for enthusiasm and desire.
- *Pink*—Symbolizes happiness, grace and gentility.
- *Pale colors*—Friendship.
- *Dark crimson*—Conveys mourning.
- *Red and yellow*—Together stand for happy feelings.
- *Red and white*—Together mean unity.
- *Single rose*—Sent in full bloom says "I love you".
- *Thornless rose*—Love at first sight.
- *Bouquet*—Sent in full bloom means gratitude.

—*Margie Wampler Butler, Pennsylvania*

**Prickly pear** cactus are hard to weed, but a long-handled barbecue fork works for me. Just insert the fork and twist. The weeds come right out. I also use clothes hangers for plant supports. Just straighten out the hanger, leaving the hook.

—*Karen Sayan, Burt, Michigan*

**Mix cornmeal** and powdered clothes detergent in an old salt shaker. After gardening, use this mix to wash your hands. It cleans the hands and makes them feel good, too.
—*Dorothy Goudie*
*Osawatomie, Kansas*

**Back problems** stopped me from lugging a 2-gallon sprayer around my 5 acres of mountain pasture. So I bought a collapsible 2-wheeled suitcase carrier for less than $10, strapped a 5-gallon bucket on it with bungee cords and set the sprayer in the bucket. The sprayer is well protected and follows me into even the tightest places. —*Carole McKee*
*Trinidad, Colorado*

**If anyone** has ever trampled on their ground-cover plants while painting the house, you probably understand the mess I created. I perked up my ground cover after a painting project by using a shop vacuum to pick up paint chips and fluff the vines and leaves. They looked refreshed and in good shape in minutes.
—*Connie Kocon*
*Erie, Pennsylvania*

**Use an aluminum** foil roasting pan for a grow light reflector. Attach it to the top of the light.
—*Ann Zawistowski*
*Blaine, Minnesota*

**Used golf club** shafts (without club heads) are very handy in the garden. I get mine from golf pro shops and other repair shops.

I use them to stake pepper plants, mark my rows and even support young trees. —*Larry DeRoche*
*Dunstable, Massachusetts*

**I water** my tomato plants right at the roots. To help save my back, I attached a long section (about 4 feet long) of 3/4-inch PVC pipe to the water hose using connectors I purchased at the hardware store. Watering wands also work well.
—*Joseph Wantz*
*Union Bridge, Maryland*

**Don't throw** old sheer curtains away. They are perfect for covering cabbage plants to keep destructive moths from laying eggs there. It is also a good cover for lettuce in hot weather. —*Lizzie Ann Schwartz*
*Mt. Perry, Ohio*

**To clean** rusty garden tools, I rub them with a steel-wool soap pad dipped in turpentine. Then I polish with wadded aluminum foil.
—*Mary Ohms, Carrollton, Texas*

**An oversized fork** and spoon make handy garden tools. The fork is perfect for loosening soil, and the spoon is good for digging holes for my plants or seeds.
—*Elsie Barton*
*Birmingham, Alabama*

**Save large salt shakers** to use as handy dispensers when it's time for planting your garden. Fill them with seeds, then shake out in neat rows.

—*Desoree Thompson*
*Cabazon, California*

**I used 2-inch PVC** pipe to make a greenhouse. Just put two rows of smaller metal pipes in the ground with the ends protruding at the surface. Then bend several pieces of PVC between the rows of metal pipes, making bows that serve as the frame for the greenhouse. Then cover the frame with plastic. When the weather warms in spring, just take the plastic off. It gives me a 3-week start on the growing season.

—*Carol Hostetter*
*Doylesburg, Pennsylvania*

**To label plants**, especially perennials, I cut large lids from margarine tubs or ice cream pails into pie-shaped wedges. Then I label with a permanent marker and stick them into the ground.

—*Rose Krushelniski*
*Nipawin, Saskatchewan*

**Keep white disposable** plastic knives and a permanent laundry marker with your garden tools. Each time you plant something, write the date and other information on the knife handle and insert the blade beside the plant or seeds. This is a real time-saver. I wish I'd known about it when I started gardening 40 years ago. —*Marilyn Fry*
*Cassopolis, Michigan*

**In fall**, pot up leftover spring flowering bulbs, water and store them in a picnic cooler in an unheated garage. Then, after 12 weeks of cold treatment, bring them indoors and place in a sunny location. They'll start growing and flower in about 4 weeks. —*Howard Baszynski*
*Wauwatosa, Wisconsin*

**To keep grass** from growing in your garden, spread newspaper five to six layers deep in the open areas. Put a thin layer of dirt on top and water down a few times. This helps the paper and soil stay in place. The paper eventually breaks down into an excellent soil additive.
—*Lena Pierce, Raceland, Louisiana*

**Place your** compost bin on a pallet with 1/2-inch hardware cloth stapled to the top. This provides plenty of air to the pile, and it's easy to shovel the compost right off the pallet when ready.

I also add a chimney of PVC pipe to my compost bins. All that's needed is a pipe (I use 4-inch pipe) that is 1 or 2 feet taller than your compost bin. Drill several holes in the pipe along the length. This will keep air circulating throughout your pile.

—*Clyde Wallenfang*
*Greenfield, Wisconsin*

# INDEX

# Plant Hardiness Zone Map

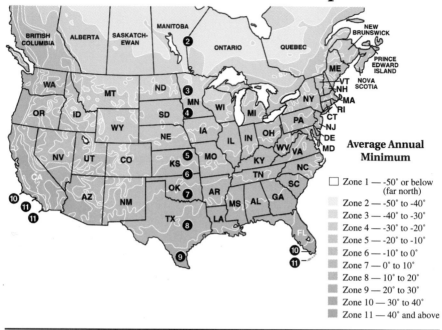

**Average Annual Minimum**

- ☐ Zone 1 — -50° or below (far north)
- Zone 2 — -50° to -40°
- Zone 3 — -40° to -30°
- Zone 4 — -30° to -20°
- Zone 5 — -20° to -10°
- Zone 6 — -10° to 0°
- Zone 7 — 0° to 10°
- Zone 8 — 10° to 20°
- Zone 9 — 20° to 30°
- Zone 10 — 30° to 40°
- Zone 11 — 40° and above